THE MOVING VIOLATION

A ROCK AND ROLL MEMOIR
1966-1968

Cover Design: Dennis Johnson and R J Furth

Interior Fleurons and Art: Kris Orenberg

Copyright 2014 Dennis Johnson and R J Furth

ISBN 13: 9781497307773

Library of Congress Control Number: 2014904749

Create Space Independent Publishing Platform

North Charleston, SC

THE MOVING VIOLATION
A ROCK AND ROLL MEMOIR
1966-1968

Dennis Johnson with R J Furth

DEDICATION, DENNIS: I'd like to dedicate this book to the four adults who, in 1967, believed in their kids and supported their desire to form a band and make a record. Without their help and kind generosity, The Moving Violation would not have been possible. A heartfelt thank you to Beverly Small, Audrey Kennedy, Jim Cain Sr., and Dr. Walter Abrams.

DEDICATION, R J. I'd to thank the many musicians who taught, encouraged, and were willing to play with me, especially, though not limited to, the following: David Zuber (my first teacher) in Colorado, Brent Huber in Tokyo, Adam Thompson and Jairus Anthony in Kuala Lumpur, Anthony Wimshurst in London, Tom McNeil and Dennis Johnson, Ann Dam and Tom Chart in Denver.

ACKNOWLEDGEMENT: Dennis and R J would like to thank all of the musicians who inspired us, past and present. This book would have been incomplete without the help of Jim Cain, Steve Crosse, Mike Kennedy, Steve Small, and Lee Abrams. We regret that Gary Harn was not alive to participate, though he was always with us in spirit.

INTRODUCTION

I had just finished playing bass on three songs as part of the duo TRON at an open mic night in Evergreen, Colorado, when a lovely, thin woman with long, wavy, reddish hair and a quick smile asked if I would back her on a few tunes. After finishing (I only remember Peggy Lee's "Fever" and a Beatles tune) she, Ann Dam Johnson, asked if I'd like to jam with her new band. Eager to find something other than a duo, I readily agreed. A week later I went to Ann's house and was introduced to Tom Chart, a keyboard player, and Ann's husband, Dennis Johnson, a guitarist who was wearing a green Chicago White Sox baseball cap. Within minutes Dennis and I discovered that we had both been born on the south side of Chicago, within a few miles of each other, only four months apart. (I'm older!) Dennis' family had moved to the southern suburbs when he was about ten, thus his support for the White Sox, a south side team. My family had moved to the northern suburbs when I was five, which is why I grew up a Chicago Cubs fan, a team whose home is on the north side of the city. In spite of our opposing sports affiliation, we discovered common ground in our love of music and shared experiences from our youth.

Over the next few months we grew closer and closer. Dennis learned that I was writing novels (for which I left a career as a high school history teacher) and asked to read some. He apparently liked my writing and wondered if I'd be interested in helping him write a memoir about his high school band and the battle of the bands they had won at Bloom High School. All of us have memories of events that shaped our lives, that helped to make us who we are today.

For some it was a sporting victory, for others it was losing their virginity or a first job or acceptance to a university. Dennis Johnson's life changed when he fell in love with music. He was 12 years old in 1963 when popular music crept under his skin and permeated his heart and never left. It started with "Sink The Bismarck", a popular tune on the radio that was featured in a film of the same name, then Dennis was hooked by the guitar playing of The Ventures. It was the arrival of the Beatles and Rolling Stones, though, that captured Dennis' soul as it did for so many young people. While many of us only dreamed of forming a band, Dennis actually did.

Whether a child of the 60s, 70s or 00s, anybody who has ever loved popular music and dreamed of being a rock star will relate to this memoir. It doesn't contain any explicit sex, and very little drugs or violence, because life in the predominantly white suburbs of Chicago in the mid 60s was idyllic. There was no AIDS, kids rode their bikes in the streets and didn't worry about kidnappings or drive-by shootings. What mattered most to many in the mid to late 60s was music, which was on radio and TV and at your local recreation center or high school gym. And the music was great! Open up YouTube and listen to the songs mentioned in this book. Absorb the energy of an era through your ears. If you're a gear-head, get online and check out the equipment that Dennis discusses. This book is the story of a young man's passion for music, a passion that continues to be a major part of Dennis Johnson's life. He is a wonderful guitar player who still gets excited about playing and talking music. Dennis and I interviewed the four surviving band members (Gary Harn passed away in 2011) and the young man (no longer young) who produced the band's 45. Interviews were conducted in Denver, St. Louis and Chicago. It's been a long process, including a 2300-mile road trip, and I've enjoyed every minute of it. Hopefully, you too will enjoy the journey that took us through half a dozen states and back 45 years.

One final point needs to be made. Dennis is a collector and he still owns many artifacts from his musical past. The cover photo is the Fender Bandmaster amplifier that he purchased in 1967. He still owns it. All of the photos, news articles and receipts featured in this memoir are still part of Dennis' collection of personal memorabilia. The fleurons used in the book were taken from The Moving Violation coat that Dennis describes in this memoir and that he still owns. Dennis does not live in the past, but he still takes immense pleasure from his memories.

R J Furth (2014)

CHAPTER ONE – FROM BUILDING MODELS TO FIRST ELECTRIC GUITAR

RICHARD JAESCHKE
ANITA JANKEVICS
BRUCE JOHNSON
DALE JOHNSON

DAVID JOHNSON
DENNIS JOHNSON
JEFFREY JOHNSON
ROBERT JOHNSTON

I was desperate to get my hands on my own electric guitar. I believe it was my mother who took me to Roberto's Music Salon on August 19, 1966, to purchase my first one. I had saved $130 working for my friend Steve's father, helping at grand openings at some of his new Checker stations, pumping gas, doing any work available for an unskilled 15-year-old. The money was folded into a wad and stuffed into my pocket. After telling Roberto my price range he pulled down a strange bell-shaped guitar. The coolest thing about the guitar was that it was a 12-string, and it had a solid body and was electric. Since I loved the Byrds and their 12-string sound, that guitar—a Danelectro 12-String Bellzouki 7010—dazzled me. It had a rich dark brown color along the outer edge that faded to beige as it neared the center of the body. The pick-guard was tortoise-shell plastic with an additional piece of tortoise-shell plastic around the pick-up. The neck had a beautiful Brazilian rosewood fret board with white dot markers. In retrospect it was not that attractive, yet to my 15-year-old eyes it was one of the most beautiful things I'd ever seen. We plugged it into an amp and I sat down to play. I was really impressed by the sound which was full and rich with incredible sustain. (Sustain is the period of time that the sound remains from first strum or pick until it becomes inaudible. If you strum a guitar and the sound lasts a long time, it has great sustain.) When I picked each individual string of a chord, it rang out beautifully. It was a unique guitar with a unique sound and I knew I wanted it. Buying that Danelectro was the culmination of a journey that started half a dozen years earlier.

In the 1950s transistor radios were the new thing. Music was suddenly very portable. It could be held in your hand, you could go to sleep with it under your pillow. I loved the transistor radio; just to hold it in my hand felt very empowering. The first song that grabbed me was "Sink The Bismarck" by Johnny Horton, which was released in 1960 to accompany the movie by the same name. (Both song and movie were based on a true British naval victory against a massive German ship in 1941.) The military beat of the song hypnotized me. My late grandfather, who had lived with us on the south side of Chicago, had left behind an old Kay guitar. Kay was a manufacturer of medium quality guitars located in Chicago. There was a closet in our house in Roseland (on the south side of the city) and there it sat, an early fifties Kay arch top. The song "Sink The Bismarck" was running through my brain and it was so cool. After all I was a nine-year-old still playing army and the song was about a major naval engagement. I had seen people playing guitar on TV and knew I had to press down on the strings with one hand and pluck the strings with my other hand. I picked up my grandfather's guitar one day and with "Sink The Bismarck" in my head I started to pluck out some notes. I used only the bottom three strings and the guitar must have been somewhat in tune. After a bit of time I could play the melody to "Sink The Bismarck". This was a very satisfying achievement for a nine-year-old who was about to be moved to the suburbs of which he knew nothing and where he had no close friends.

In 1961 we moved twenty miles south of Roseland to Chicago Heights. Rather than the old section of Chicago Heights, which was first settled in 1833, we moved to a new part called Olympia Terrace that had recently been a tomato field. Olympia Terrace featured new roads, a new elementary school and no trees. To make matters worse, most of the families that moved into Olympia Terrace were young with kids much younger than me. This was a huge disappointment because Roseland had lots of old trees and a sense of community, and I had left many friends behind. I remember this as a lonely time as it took a while for me to find kids my own age to whom I could relate. Life wasn't all bad in Olympia Terrace, though, in part because there was a strip mall nearby that had a shop where I spent a lot of my time and money. Gay-Time Sports and Hobby was a mom-and-pop store, though I called it Stone's hobby shop because the owner was Harold Stone. (How times have changed. The same name today would lead people to think it was a shop for homosexuals. In the 60s the theme song for *The Flintstones* promised viewers that they would, "have a gay old time".) Harold ran the store along with his wife and son Greg. Greg was a few years older than me, though not more mature. We shared a love of slot carts and Soupy Sales (TV comedian) and music. Greg lived just a couple blocks away and he was my saving grace. Suddenly life wasn't boring for me. The fact that his parents owned the hobby shop was certainly fun. We would sometimes help around the store and Greg's parents would let us pick out something for payment. (Around '63, I picked out a skateboard, certainly one of the first ones in Chicago.) My friendship with Greg also had a minor musical component as his older step-brother turned us on to some music, including *West Side Story*. All of these little pieces, over time, would add up.

Like many young people in the early 60s, I joined Columbia Record Club. You would pay a few cents to receive six records, then agree to buy more at the full price. The first records I bought included *West Side Story* and Ray Charles' *Greatest Hits*. Greg and I also listened to The Beach Boys and Jan and Dean, but the most amazing group to us was the Ventures, an instrumental group formed in 1958 in Tacoma, Washington. My first album of theirs, which was one of my initial orders from the Columbia Record Club in very early '63, was *The Ventures play Telstar and The Lonely Bull*. The Ventures were the first group to use a fuzz-tone effect on guitar. They started out playing Fenders and were pictured on the album cover with three of them: lead guitar, rhythm guitar, and electric bass guitar. Their drummer was quite good, a real pro who kept a steady, driving beat. That album features the first known use of a flanger (special effect which 'colors' the sound) on a guitar. Red Rhoads, a session steel guitar player who helped the Ventures in the studio from time to time, was an early innovator in developing special effects. He had made a special fuzz distortion box and the Ventures were the first to use it on a recorded song ("2000 Pound Bee") in 1962. They also were the first to record using the reverse tracking method. (The Beatles made the sound popular with *Revolver* as well as on later albums. "Rain" has a good example of reverse tracking at the end of that song.). The Ventures were a huge influence on my developing musical tastes because of their use of guitars and with lead guitar on every song. Wow! They set the standard for rock electric guitar playing for the first half of the '60s. I think it was their focus on guitar and creating such cool sounds that grabbed us, plus there were no dumb lyrics or other distractions. It was pure music.

I had a little record player that I kept in my bedroom and I remember even at that age being told to turn it down. We really got into the music, with Greg digging the bass parts and me getting into the lead parts. We took turns goofing around on the Kay arch top guitar in my basement, a great place to hang out on hot, humid summer days. We'd goof around building models and racing slot cars and watching Soupy Sales, but we kept coming back to the music. It was exciting and we knew there was something there. We knew it would be cool to play an instrument and we talked about forming a band, though at that point it was just kid talk.

I remember watching a Jack Parr *Tonight* show on TV in late 1963 that showed the Beatles performing in London to thousands of screaming girls. We were not that impressed because we were still into the Ventures who played their instruments well, but as '64 rolled along our opinions changed. About this time I met a kid named Ross who was in my 8th-grade homeroom class. Ross and his older brother were in a band called The Fugitives. I went to his house once to see the band's equipment and I was in complete awe of it. The Fugitives played sock hops at school (dances where kids took off their shoes and danced in their socks) and local dances that were sometimes held at churches. Ross was a popular guy (with a girlfriend with whom he supposedly went to third base) and his band was popular, and I was taking mental notes. The Fugitives even put out a 45 rpm record, both sides being instrumentals. Building plastic models and racing slot cars began to fall by the wayside as I slowly realized that music might lead to more exciting hobbies, particularly girls.

In April when I turned fourteen I received a little Mayfair tape recorder. I think it was from Walgreens in Chicago Heights. Walgreens was important because it was near my church; on Sundays, Steve Small (much more on Steve later) and I would ditch church to hang out at Walgreens eating fries, drinking cokes and reading music magazines. *Hit Parader* was a favorite magazine because it had lyrics to the popular songs of the day. Thanks to bicycles we were mobile. Bike trips began getting longer, and the previous year we had discovered a great record store in the old section of Chicago Heights called Co-op Records, which had a great selection of 45s and albums. We liked to just hang out there checking the new records that had been released. In the fall of '64 I bought the 45 of the Animals' "House of the Rising Sun". I also bought the Animals' first LP for Greg's birthday. It was a cool album with some blues songs I'd never heard before, and by the time school started that fall I was getting into guitar a lot.

Although I lived in the northern section of Chicago Heights, our house fell in the Flossmoor school district. All my good friends went to Bloom High School while I attended Homewood-Flossmoor High. Bloom was racially mixed, bigger and better at sports, and even had a few all black bands. (The Jaywalkers would compete against my group in the same Battle of the Bands a few years later.) Homewood-Flossmoor was all white, including a large Jewish population that had fled the south side of Chicago after World War II as more blacks moved into that area. I felt inferior to my classmates at Homewood-Flossmoor, mainly because my parents always told me that we were poor compared to most people who lived in Flossmoor. Since Greg Stone lived near me, I felt more comfortable with him and his parents as well as Steve Small, the kid I knew from church. Steve, Greg and I would play softball on local fields, as did so many young teenagers in America. It didn't matter that some of the kids came from wealthy families, I could relate better to kids from the Heights. It seemed to me that there was some kind of caste system at work at Homewood-Flossmoor and I was on the lowest rung. Fortunately, I got to hang out with my friends on the weekends and our social life began to revolve around church. As much as my friends and I didn't care for church, it provided us with a different social scene. Besides confirmation class, our church had two sports teams for junior high kids. That was my saving grace, which is kind of ironic since we weren't very religious. We had lots of great times through the church, then on Mondays I was back at the Flossmoor schools. Drat! I really didn't care about anything in school, it was a distraction from what was really important to me: playing music, thinking of sex, and being with my friends in the Heights. At Homewood-Flossmoor I was a witness more than a participant. The Rolling Stone's tune "(I Can't Get No) Satisfaction", released in the summer of 1965 at the start of my freshman year, really spoke to me.

Greg Stone, Steve Small, birthday boy Dennis (April '65)

In February of '65 I started taking guitar lessons at a very straight music school in Chicago Heights. It was a six-lesson package with a guitar that they lent you, all for a grand total of $15. My teacher was older and these lessons were a real turnoff since they were for novice musicians rather than serious musicians. The guitar they offered was terrible as well, a real piece of crap. I realized it was up to me to figure out the guitar. That summer pop music had a breakthrough in guitar sounds. "Satisfaction" had a buzzing tone that blew our minds. I tried to mimic the sound by weaving tissue paper through the strings of my Kay. (I hadn't heard of a fuzz tone although the Ventures used one in 1964. Like many young guitarists I was unaware of the technology that existed, so I tried to recreate it with low tech.) I really had the bug now and all I could think about was music and girls. Unlike Ross who had a real, live girlfriend, all I had was some adult magazines I had bought at Jimmy's Newsstand in downtown Chicago Heights.

I tried sports at Homewood-Flossmoor in hopes of attracting girls, but I was terrible in football and ended up as a fourth stringer. I had more luck with wrestling and was doing well in the 165 pound class when my world came tumbling down, literally. I was practicing takedowns one day when my 180-pound partner—John Sutoris, a big, blonde guy— came down on my ankle, crushing it in three places. I was in the hospital for a week, which is when I realized that playing sports was just not my forte. While I was recovering with a full leg cast I decided to focus on the guitar. The Beatles' *Rubber Soul* was released in December of '65, and in early '66 I picked up a song book of the album that had a chord diagram above the lyrics where the chords appeared in the song. This was the most helpful thing I'd seen and it was how I learned to play along with the words to a song. This was huge. Now the craving for an electric guitar was almost unbearable. This craving, combined with the fact that I was still recovering from my wrestling injury, confirmed that sports was now consigned to the same part of my past as building models and racing slot cars. Music was safer and far more likely to attract females than my youthful fondness for things you could find at Gay-Time Sports and Hobby. Chicks (as we called girls in those days) seemed attracted to guys who were in bands, even local bands.

Speaking of girls, while in middle school and during freshman year I did go to the occasional sock hop or dance, and like most boys my age I had high hopes, though little real idea regarding what it was I was hoping for. Like Elvis Costello's song "Mystery Dance" says, "I was working on mysteries without any clues". In truth, like most boys my age, I was a wall-flower and never participated in any make-out parties that people were talking about. My self-esteem was particularly low after having been pushed around in a wheelchair during the second half of my freshman year. I had also, not surprisingly, put on weight while incapacitated. Still, I attended many dances and sock hops, and though I didn't have any "girlie action" (as the Stones called it) I did get to listen to bands, which I thought were very cool. There were also a lot of dances at Temple Anshe Sholom, which had a large, comfortable hall. Howie Rosen belonged to the temple, and later when we formed our band, The Moving Violation, we used to joke that, "Howie's working on the temple," meaning he was going to get us a job there. He did become a fan of our band and did, in fact, get us an engagement there in early '67.

In June '66, a neighborhood girl had a party where a local group, The NOYB, played in front of her garage. This was like a slice of heaven for me. Just two doors up from my house was a live band playing electric guitars with amps and drums! The NOYB were just starting out and would become The Faintest Idea. I knew a few of the guys in the band: Jeff on bass and Greg M on guitar. So there were Steve and I, in our own neighborhood, checking out The NOYB, telling ourselves, "We can do this." All we needed was equipment. If you had equipment—electric guitars, amplifiers and microphones—you could have a music group. The Byrds were a group that we liked a lot and their leader, Roger McGuinn, used an electric 12-string guitar. The Beatles had used electric 12-strings on many of their songs and now the Byrds were taking folk songs—particularly by Bob Dylan—and putting them to a

14

rock beat with electric guitar, featuring the unique jangle of the 12-string. This was the beginning of the folk rock sound, which was huge in 1966.

There was a record store nearby in Park Forest that had live bands performing on Sunday afternoons. One Sunday afternoon in July, I went there and sang a song with a band (maybe The NOYB or some members from it). I sang The Animals' "We Gotta Get Outta This Place". I did pretty well and surprisingly felt no fear. In fact, it felt pretty great, which was odd because I didn't sing again in a group until many years later. Still, I now knew what it was like to perform, and this feeling propelled me to buy my first electric guitar. I wasn't alone with my rock and roll dreams. Steve Small also loved music, though he claims today that he has no natural musical talent. Everybody played tonette in Steve's elementary school. A tonette was a plastic flute that was, for many, their introduction to musical instruments. Steve's fifth grade class held a tonette concert for parents, and Steve remembers not being invited to play because he wasn't good enough. This usually meant that the failed tonette player had no future as a musician. Steve tried trumpet, with no greater success, but refused to give up his musical dreams. His parents bought him a Kay classical guitar around sixth grade, but Steve never became proficient with that instrument.

Steve and I had played together on a church basketball team, though we weren't friends yet. Basketball brought us closer together, but it was the Methodist church that sealed our friendship. Well, not actually attending Methodist church, but activities sponsored by the church. We had confirmation class together and a

15

week-long summer Bible study. The Bible study had a music component in which we discovered that we shared a love of the Beach Boys and The Ventures. We spent a lot of time in the Methodist Youth Fellowship, though some of our fondest memories are of ditching church and riding our bikes around Chicago Heights. Steve had bought a Kay guitar and was desperate to be in a band, yet didn't believe he would ever play guitar as well as I did. The logical conclusion was to drop the guitar and buy a bass, which had only four strings to the guitar's six, and which took much less skill to play. Steve never took a bass lesson, but he knew something about notes and chords from his tonette, trumpet and guitar playing; given enough time he could figure out which notes to play. Steve and I began to play together, basic tunes that were popular at the time such as "Louie Louie". Soon, though, we had the urge to expand and form a real band.

An important aside regarding Steve's musical skills: After graduating from Brown University Steve spent a couple of years in Munich, Germany, playing pedal steel guitar in professional bands. The pedal steel is a very complex instrument that requires the use of both hands, feet and knees; Steve claims he only became good through hours and hours of practice. Perhaps, but I'm still very impressed.

Mike Kennedy attended the Presbyterian Church, but he lived in the same neighborhood in Chicago Heights as Steve Small, though they weren't close friends. When freshman year began at Bloom high school Steve and Mike became closer, hanging out, talking about the new TV show, *Batman*. At some point Steve went to Mike's house and was stunned by what he saw. There, sitting in the living room was a sparkling, purple Beverley drum kit. Steve had never seen a drum kit and its magnificence blew him away. Attending Homewood-Flossmoor, I wasn't part of the Bloom social scene, so I wasn't with Steve when he first saw Mike's kit. Eventually, though, Steve introduced me to Mike. Although we came from different feeder schools (the middle schools that feed into high schools) we soon discovered that we had a mutual interest in music, as did most young people in 1965. Most important, Mike was eager to play and had been practicing along to his mother's hi-fi. Steve brought me to Mike's house to see the drum set. We were all into the Rolling Stones; one of our favorite songs was "Paint It Black", which had been released that May. After hearing Mike play this tune accompanied by the record, I thought, "Here is our drummer." He just nailed that tune. About the same time Steve bought a Kent bass from Jeff Currier of The NOYB. He also found and purchased a Magnatone bass amp. We had the basic components of a real rock and roll band. Now I was desperate to get my hands on my own electric guitar.

Robertos was a new music store in the area and it seemed different from other music stores. In those days most music stores were stodgy, traditional shops, aimed at the entire family. Besides pianos, they sold band instruments such as trumpets, clarinets, violins and probably tonettes. Electric guitars and basses were not their thing. Roberto Elam, on the other hand, was in his thirties and was somewhat hip— at least hipper than just about anybody else in the neighborhood. He was of medium build, darker- skinned than most in the area (he might have had Italian or Hispanic blood), though it didn't matter. What mattered was that he was friendly and, more important, he would be a major sponsor of the 1967 Bloom Battle of the Bands. He carried acoustic and electric guitars, basses, drum kits and accessories for drums, everything a young band could want except Fender products. Roberto was quite a salesman and could cut you a great deal, according to him. He definitely would not try to rip you off. I had never heard of the Danelectro brand, but when he took it off the shelf and handed it to me, it was love at first sight. Later I read that Danelectro made guitars for Sears, their Silvertone line. A few years earlier you could catch me drooling over Silvertones in the Sears catalogues as if the guitars were lingerie models. Now I was holding one (the guitar, not the lingerie model). While it was well made, the materials for the guitar were on the less expensive side: Masonite, poplar and maple for the neck. The neck was fairly decent, being wider than the Rickenbacker, easier for placing your left hand for chording. (A narrow neck means the strings are closer together, which means your fingers are forced closer together when you make chords.)

$_____ _____ _____ august 19 19 66

Received from _____ Dennis Johnson _____

_____ One hundred nine +once Dollars 100

/— Danelctro twelve strings _____

No. _____ _____ N. E.

There weren't many 12-string guitars around at this time, though many popular songs used 12-strings including The Rolling Stones' "As Time Goes By", The Beatles' "Hard Day's Night", The Byrds' "Mr. Tambourine Man" and "Eight Miles High". The 12-string sound was new and exciting, and the fact that the Danelectro was $109 out the door, including taxes and a case, was a no-brainer for me. I could not have been happier.

I also realized that I needed something else to go along with this guitar: an amp. The Chicago Heights Symphony of Music, where I had taken lessons the previous year, would rent equipment. At $15 for three months, they rented me a Gibson Explorer amp with reverb and tremolo. It had a 10-inch speaker and was rated at 35 watts, good enough to start making loud music. Now the three core players—Mike Kennedy, Steve Small and myself—had their own equipment and we started playing together. Naturally we attempted the simplest songs first. "Louie Louie", a repetitive three-chord tune, was a staple with most local bands and had been around for a few years. The Shadows of Night, a local band, had a hit with Van Morrison's "Gloria", another three-chorder, and we soon learned it. That was the summer of '66 and I was finally in a band. Goodbye childhood, hello adolescence.

Me, the Danelectro and my Fender Bandmaster

In August of '66 we started practicing pretty seriously at Mike Kennedy's house. Mike was average height with long, wavy, blond hair. He had a deep voice, almost baritone, which was surprising for such a slender guy. Mike lived on 15th Street in Ashland Park, an older section of Chicago Heights. His dad had passed away when Mike was young and his older sister was married, so it was just Mike and his mom Audrey. Mike was more laid back than Steve Small yet wilder than either of us, which might be a drummer thing. He was an excellent ice skater and when they flooded the park across the street to make a skating rink he was in his element, chasing girls on the ice and putting snow down their pants, which we called snow balling. Mike didn't have a girlfriend when we met, but soon hooked up with a girl who had moved in from Indiana. He was a very private person who didn't share his feelings with us, though he apparently shared them with his girlfriend. Mike spent a lot of time with his mom, who worked full-time at the Chicago Heights Star, the local newspaper. Audrey was a big supporter of the band and she let us practice at their house Friday nights and during the day on Saturday.

The song that defined us at the start was the Stones' "Paint It Black". Mike really had the drum part down and although we didn't play it in public until the end of the year, it was a bunch of fun to play. It sounded particularly good on my new 12-String Danelectro, a real full sound as the Stones had meant it to be. We also worked on other Stones songs: "Satisfaction", "The Last Time", and "Play With Fire", which was the B-side of "The Last Time". We also learned The Kinks' "You Really Got Me", "Little Latin Lupe Lu" (written by Bill Medley of the Righteous Brothers), and other songs that had simple chord patterns, like "House of the Rising Sun". We had limited practice time as school had just started and Steve had cross-country practice. Besides, nobody could drive yet so we got together only about once a week at the most, and sometimes even less.

Steve Small had a round face and dark hair. When he wore his dark-rimmed glasses, he looked almost Oriental, which became an inside joke. He was a skinny guy and we accidentally broke his collarbone once goofing around, another source of inside jokes. Although Steve went to Bloom High School, we became close friends. I knew that he was in all the smart classes and some people thought he was cocky, but he had a lot of self-confidence and he was very positive about his, and our band's, future. Steve was my smartest friend, and he would be the only person I was close with who went to an Ivy League school, Brown. Steve lived on Franklin Street in an older part of Chicago Heights that had a lot of trees. His family was wealthy, though he never flaunted it. His mother, Beverly was a social worker, liberal and open minded; she marched with Martin Luther King, Jr., which was very progressive and rare in our neighborhood. Beverly was a role model for Steve and a huge supporter of our bands. She drove us around to early performances and paid us $25 for our first job, which was a party in the Small's basement for Steve's sister Marsha. Steve was a huge part of my life when the bands were happening; I looked to him for advice and trusted that advice, and I still do to this day.

Paul Revere and the Raiders were a hot band at this time, an apparently funny group of guys, though in hindsight I now realize that their image had been carefully crafted by management. Ever since the Beatles released their movie *A Hard Day's Night* in 1964—a zany film that portrayed the Beatles as irreverent, wacky guys—fun became a sub-genre of music. The television show *Where The Action Is,* a Dick Clark Production which ran 1965-67, featured Paul Revere and The Raiders who dressed in the

22

Revolutionary-era clothes of the original Paul Revere, early hero of the American Revolution. Wearing three-cornered hats trimmed in white feathers, long, braided red or blue coats, and white riding pants tucked into black riding boots (red, white and blue; Paul Revere's ride), the band members were energetic and always smiling. (In 1967 the ultimate 'fun' band was created as part of a new television show that successfully banked on the idea of zany rock and roll: *The Monkees*.) It was because we liked Paul Revere and The Raiders that we decided to pattern ourselves after them, and why we named the group The Midnite Ryders.

In those days most of us were restricted as to when we could go out: never on a school night or the night before school, except for church activities. Steve and I belonged to a church which had a youth group known as MYF: Methodist Youth Fellowship. We took advantage of MYF to get out of the house on a Sunday night. Another motivation might have been Jeannie Kendal and a few other girls who belonged to MYF. It was through this organization that we would get our first gig. Steve and I were fairly active in MYF, which had a new assistant minister by the name of Harry Cho. I think Harry was Korean and we used to make fun of his accent. (Ethnic humor was popular in the 60s with Buddy Hackett and Jerry Lewis doing wretched Chinese accents and Bill Dana doing a Latino Jose Jimenez.) Harry would say things like, "You guys good 'nuf be on Ed Sullivan show." He was a nice guy and we took advantage of him and pretty much controlled what went on at MYF. As assistant minister, Harry was in charge of youth activities. There was another guitar player in MYF who was in a band called Isle of Blue, so we decided to have a Halloween party at MYF—with

Harry's full support—with our groups as the entertainment. Steve, Mike and I got Greg Price and Ronnie Evans to join us. I rode the school bus with Greg and Ronnie and used to go to Greg's house because he had a sonic blue Fender Mustang guitar, a quality guitar in my opinion at the time. It was way out of my price range (a couple of hundred bucks was a lot of money in those days) but I knew I would own a Fender one day. Ronnie had a full head of blond hair and he would prance around sometimes in a way that reminded me of Mark Lindsey, the vocalist and front man of Paul Revere. Ronnie was a vocalist and I thought the girls would go gaga over him, so we ended up forming The Midnite Ryders to play the MYF gig. That was a switch from the norm, which is to form a band, then find gigs.

Both groups, The Isle of Blue and The Midnite Ryders, shared equipment at the MYF gig. In those days it was all very low tech and we sang out of guitar amps. We agreed to play five songs each in order to fairly share the gig, then another ten songs each twice for a total of 25 songs per group. It was necessary to play songs twice because we hadn't had time to learn that many songs. We had no idea how long it would actually take to play 25 songs, with time between songs. As it turned out we ran out of time and never played nearly that many. We brought Christmas tree lights from Steve's basement and a spotlight that changed colors as it rotated. With the house lights off this created a pretty cool effect. I don't remember being nervous, nor do I remember us being nervous for any gigs after that. Steve, Mike and I were always confident in our playing and it showed. Some people would take that for being conceited, but we were just confident. We had practiced a few times with Greg Price and Ronnie Evans, and we were sure we would be better than The Isle of Blue.

Mike Kennedy, Steve Small and I, the core members of the group, were in charge of song selection. There was never any argument about what to play. If somebody suggested a popular tune, we'd all work on it until we were ready to perform it. In fact, there was no leader; The Midnite Ryders were a band of equals, of friends. The dynamics did not change when we added Greg and Ronnie. Of course, we needed Ronnie Evan's in-put as he was the one who was singing. I believe Ronnie also helped write an instrumental, "The Midnight Ride". Other than that, the core three were in charge, with Steve and me being the driving force for this job since it was in our church. This first show was an opportunity that we created in order to see how we would perform in front of a live audience. The fact that we never played again as the Midnite Ryders reveals that Greg and Ronnie didn't click with the core members. Although it was good for a start, this line-up didn't create the sound and feel that we were seeking. We would, however, soon find the rest of the group that would become The Moving Violation.

I had a major role in figuring out the songs since I was the lead player. I had to first know the chords, then figure out some kind of lead part for the break in the song, then make sure everyone else had some idea of what they were doing. A song like "The Last Time" by the Stones is a good example. It starts with a riff which I had to figure out, then the drums came in (a beat in this case). Next, the bass and guitar entered following the chords to the song. There are four different chords and a couple of places where everything drops out except the lead guitar and drum beat. We would talk about it, but since I was the lead player and started the song, I was kind of the leader of the whole thing, at least on that song. That's how it would worked in those very early days before Jim Cain and Gary Harn, the other members of The Moving Violation, came along. I didn't do note-for-note leads. In fact my leads were called fake-outs. A fake-out was me taking a lead part and making it my own. Since my ear was not developed enough to copy lead parts note-for-note, I became an improviser. I have relied on this for my entire career as a lead player. It's interesting that what started as an inadequacy eventually led to my proficiency as a lead player. So within the group I became a musical leader (along with Steve) while outside the group I was more of a follower. Looking back, I realize that I was much more assertive in my Chicago Heights neighborhood where I was comfortable than at Homewood-Flossmoor High School. It was like I led two lives, with my life in the band and Chicago Heights being my favorite.

The hall where we played in the church was about the size of half a basketball court, maybe a little bigger, with at least a 12-foot ceiling. The floor was painted cement. The combination of high ceiling and concrete floor created a reverb effect because the sound bounced around a bit. That was probably a good thing for us as it helped make the sound a littler thicker. Although it was a Halloween concert, I was not aware of many kids in costumes, probably because I was totally into the music. We did not wear costumes as a band, though I might have worn a Ringo hat. (More on that later.) There were teens and pre-teens and some adults attending the party, and there was definitely no booze, drugs or sex. This was, after all, a

26

church, and it was the mid '60s. We only practiced a couple of times in Mike's living room, yet we played well with only a few noticeable blunders.

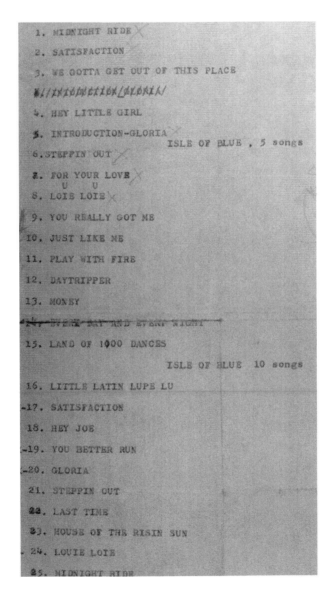

Midnite Ryders Set List Halloween '66 (Notice repeats)

The first song we played at the Halloween gig was "The Midnight Ride", an original instrumental we wrote with a descending chord pattern like the Ventures. *The Midnight Ride* was the name of Paul Revere and The Raiders' second album. We followed with the Stones' "Satisfaction", The Animals' "We Gotta Get Out of This Place", "You Really Got Me" by the Kinks, and "Just Like Me" by Paul Revere and The Raiders, which was one of our strongest songs. After The Isle of Blue's five-song set we played another five songs that started with "Gloria" (recorded by the group Them with their vocalist Van Morrison, and made popular locally by The Shadows of Night), a couple more Stones tunes, and a Young Rascals' tune, "You Better Run". I remember that we also did that party favorite, "Louie Louie". After the gig we were in a great mood, having pulled off the Halloween show. There was no money involved, and nobody had given money a thought. It wasn't about the money; it was pure fun and excitement. The feeling that we had played better than the Isle of Blue, and hopefully impressed some girls, was enough for us.

CHAPTER THREE - BIRTH OF THE MOVING VIOLATION

Gary, Jim, Mike, Steve, Dennis (January '67, Mike's house)

Although the Halloween show was a huge success—as a first job for teenagers—we knew we could be far better as a band. Ronnie Evans and Greg Price had been added for the Halloween show because they were available and Greg had an electric guitar. But they didn't have 'it', whatever 'it' was. Being in a band is sort of like dating. Although you might have a good time with your date, sometimes you know there's no future because you don't truly click on a higher level. For a band to work, everybody has to click at that higher level; your heart yearns for a long-term relationship with that group of musicians. We didn't feel the desire to 'go steady' with Ronnie and Greg. We liked them personally, but in terms of music they were soon forgotten after the Halloween show. A few weeks passed when fate stepped in and introduced the three core members (Steve, Mike and me) to our musical soul mates.

Steve and Howie Rosen were riding the school bus, talking about listening to music and playing music, and Howie asked how the band was going. "It's not going," said Steve. "We've lost our singer and guitar player." They were overheard by a girl named Karen Harn who was sitting on the bench behind them. "Hey, my brother is looking for a band." Karen mentioned that her brother Gary and his friend Jim, a guitar player, were looking for people to play with. It was one of those magic moments you read about, like when Keith Richards and Mick Jagger met on a train platform in London or when Neil Young and Stephen Stills drove past each other in L.A. (Stills recognized the hearse that Young drove) and hooked up to form Buffalo Springfield. Call it kismet or fate, we called it amazing luck. Had Karen sat in a different seat or Steve and Howie had been discussing math homework, things would have worked out differently. Instead, the final link had been made in what would become The Moving Violation. Phone numbers were exchanged, and Steve connected with Jim and Gary.

Gary Harn and Jim Cain were seniors at Rich Central High School. (Karen Harn went to Bloom because the Harn family had relocated to just within the Bloom boundary.) Jim and Gary had been in different feeder schools and had only met freshman year, possibly on the school bus. It was serendipity that put them together. Before they were old enough to drive, Gary and Jim used to walk together a lot and they would sing Beatles songs and other hit tunes as they walked. They just naturally fell into the harmonies and enjoyed trying to sound like the Beatles. Gary was tall and thin, with light brown hair; he wore dark-rimmed glasses. He was a quiet kid with a calm disposition. I never heard Gary get into an argument or say rude things about anybody (with the exception of Bob Schmit; more on that later). He was a very nice person. Jim was shorter and had brown hair. He was a bit more intense than Gary and would be involved in some conflicts toward the end of The Moving Violation's brief existence.

It was a cold Saturday in late November, '66, (in Chicago, it's always a cold November).We all met up to practice at Mike's house, the place where we were always welcome. One thing that illustrates the fact that we five musicians weren't friends is that Mike wouldn't open the door for Gary Harn because he didn't know him, and Gary, as a vocalist, didn't carry any equipment. It wasn't until Jim showed up with his guitar and amp, and vouched for Gary, that Mike let him into his house. That we didn't all know each other and yet wanted to form a band was not that unusual. Neither the Beatles nor the Rolling Stones were made up of close friends. Some knew each other from school, others were recruited or added over time. The same was true of those who would become The Moving Violation.

My amp rental had expired so I played through another amp, either Jim's amp or Steve's Magnatone bass amp. Vocals went through a guitar amp as well, a very low tech setup. Compared to today's high tech equipment, it would have sounded distorted and muffled, but to us it sounded amazing. Here were two guys— Jim Cain and Gary Harn—who knew how to sing and how to harmonize. It must have sounded good enough to Jim and Gary because they returned for another practice and we had a band. The core three were thrilled with the new additions: vocalists and musicians who brought a batch of songs that they taught us right from the beginning. As well, Jim knew a bunch of chords that I didn't know, and since his father was a guitar player Jim could go to him for help on chord progressions or to work out a difficult song. This proved to be an important resource. Jim also had an extra amp that I used until I figured out how to buy my own amp. As is true in music and sports, the addition of new members with high skill levels leads the original members to work harder and improve their skill set. Jim and Gary were good singers, and Jim was a fine guitar player, which inspired Mike, Steve and me to put more time and effort into our music. With the boost of better vocals, harmonies, and improved musicianship, we immediately began to produce better quality music. As to band dynamics and politics, things were smooth from the start. Jim and Gary were joining our band, they did not come with an agenda, did not try to take control because they were seniors and we were sophomores. There was mutual respect for fellow musicians and a fondness for the same tunes.

Jim started playing guitar at 15 and was helped by his father, who could play any stringed instrument. Jim's grandfather had been a music professor, so Jim's dad was raised with music. Unfortunately, in Jim's words, his dad was, "a musical genius, but he was not that bright in life and he tossed aside a full musical scholarship to college." He played violin at the age of 3, could play piano and guitar, but never played with a band except in the army. There were no instruments in the house when Jim was growing up, no encouragement to play, so he had to approach his dad about buying an instrument. They went to a music store and bought a Gibson SG guitar, a cherry red beauty. Jim doesn't like to talk about his dad, and it's understandable. His dad would buy Jim guitars, then sell them without telling Jim, often coming up with weak excuses such as the neck of the guitar was warped, a complete fabrication. Jim would come home from school and his guitar would be gone. In spite of his dad's personal problems, the man did show Jim how to play guitar, including barre chords, which is an easier method for playing a wide variety of chords on an electric guitar. (Barre chords can be used on acoustic guitars, but they are much harder to play.) Once he had the guitar, Jim also bought a Mel Bay guitar book that had a chart showing how to form every chord, and a Beatles song book which listed chords for each song. Between the two books he soon became a proficient rhythm guitar player who could figure out most popular songs. Jim enjoyed music so much that he let his school work slip. In his own words, "I was a horrible student. I never brought home a book in four years of high school." Music became the most important thing in Jim's life, perhaps inevitably considering his father and grandfather's musical backgrounds. When the call came to join The Midnite Ryders, he jumped at the opportunity.

Jim remembers that I showed up for their first practice wearing a Ringo hat, something I would often wear during the early practices at Mike's house, a hip fashion statement at the time as the Beatles were at their peak of popularity. (The hat was actually called a Newsboy in England and had been around for many years; when Ringo began wearing one—particularly in the Beatles films *A Hard Days Night* and *Help*—it became fashionable worldwide. You can see Newsboy hats in Austin Powers movies.) The first thing we showed Jim and Gary was our original instrumental, "Midnight Ride". We played the tune, it clicked, and we were a five-piece band.

The addition of Jim and Gary brought another huge benefit to the core group, all of whom were 15 years old: Jim was a senior, and he had a car. This was a dream-come-true for me as it meant more freedom than I'd ever experienced before. All at once I had a band with lots of potential and we had the mobility that would lead to more fun, something immensely important when you're fifteen. As well, age matters more when you're in school, and most high schoolers hang out with people of the same age. It was cool for us 15-year-olds to be hanging with two guys who were older and two grades ahead of us in school. We might have stood a little taller, gained a bit more confidence, knowing we were sophomores accepted by these two seniors. More important, we also now had the sound that was popular at the time. A band with an electric 12-string for lead was very hip in the mid '60s and it defined us for the next year. I wore the Ringo hat and I had also seen George Harrison wearing a vest on the back cover of Rubber Soul. I loved the look, so I started wearing my grandfather's vest with my button-down shirts and now I was cool, at least in my own mind.

Christmas vacation was approaching, which meant more time for fun and practice. I also did some work for Steve's father at the Checker warehouse, which gave me the opportunity to earn money for a new amp. Steve's mother Bev asked us to play at a Christmas party. She paid us $20, making it the first job for our new lineup. We were thrilled. We played in the Small's finished basement with a few Christmas lights setting the mood. The first song we played was Buddy Holly's "Not Fade Away". Jim remembers that we went for a dramatic touch with lights turned down until the first chords were struck, then the lights were turned on with a flourish. Although we were paid $4 each to play to a bunch of kids and some parents in a basement, we couldn't have been happier. People were up and dancing to our music, telling us how good we sounded. It was all the encouragement we needed to devote ourselves to making the band work.

We practiced at Mike's, and Steve's parents had hired us for the Christmas party, but the fact is that most of our parents, including my own, were not supportive of us and never came to our shows. Although Jim's dad was great for musical help, his supply of amps and guitars varied as he hocked them according to his financial needs. Parental support was nice if you were fortunate enough to have it, but most parents saw rock music as a hobby or passing phase not to be taken seriously. Ultimately, it wasn't important as long as parents weren't actively opposed to having their kids play in a rock band. At this point in my life I was totally into music and my grades suffered. I always felt that school was a burden that got in the way of what was really important to me: music. The school year would start out okay, then I would do next to nothing and quickly fall behind in my classes. I was getting Ds and C minuses, barely passing. 60% of the time my mind was on music; the other 40% was occupied thinking of girls. I loved being in my own world, the world of rock and roll dreams, which had nothing to do with high school. Adding to my disaffection with school was that we all went to different high schools. Jim and Gary were seniors at Rich Central High School, Mike and Steve were sophomores at Bloom, I was a sophomore at Homewood-Flossmoor; so I was not eager to attend. Who in their right mind would prefer sitting in Math or United States History for an hour rather than practicing in a hot, hip 5-piece band? I knew at the time that academics would never figure in my career choice.

Some might wonder whether I would have done better in school if I hadn't become hooked on music. The truth is that I was never turned on by academics and never liked being at school. To add to my educational dysfunction, I was suspended from Homewood-Flossmoor the week before Christmas for starting a food fight in the school's cafeteria. I was still overweight, didn't have a girlfriend, and didn't fit in at Homewood-Flossmoor, and I suppose I started the food fight to get attention. In point of fact, I did not plan the food fight, I just stumbled into it. When I walked into the cafeteria I saw that a lot of people were buying pint cartons of milk, six or seven at a time, which make dandy (and wet) projectiles. There were a bunch of deans in the room and nothing was happening, but the room was tense with anticipation. I guess I became impatient waiting for some action. I took the empty milk carton off my tray and whipped it across the room, hitting one of the deans in the back of the head. Immediately the air was filled with flying food and milk cartons, few of which were empty. The school claimed that there was over $400 in damage including dry-cleaning bills. Of course, this didn't sit well with my parents. They grounded me for a while but lightened up as Christmas rolled around. It wasn't that my parents were lax when it came to discipline; they apparently didn't think that a food fight was a serious offense and they weren't the type of people to hold grudges. After leaving the dean's office I went back to class where the teacher was at the board diagramming the dynamics of a food fight. I entered to the sound of applause, which at the time seemed to be worth the week's suspension. The food fight earned me some notoriety at school and I was more popular for a while because of it, but the food fight did not define me. The thing that drove me, that would define me, was music.

We started to put more time into practice and began to focus more on songs and bands that would inspire us. The first song that truly clicked for our expanded lineup was "Mr. Spaceman" by The Byrds. This was our first foray into country-rock, a new genre that was pioneered by The Byrds, Buffalo Springfield and The Eagles. "Mr. Spaceman" was surprisingly easy for us as my 12-string guitar matched Roger McGuinn's 12-string sound of The Byrds, and the harmonies of Jim and Gary approximated the harmonies of McGuinn, David Crosby and the rest of The Byrds. The song was on The Byrds album *Fifth Dimension* and released as a single in late '66. Although it was not a big hit, the song suited our style.

We were also inspired by local bands, in particular The Saints. One of the bonuses about Jim having a car is that he could drive to local gigs. One night he took us to see The Saints who were playing a dance at a VFW hall. (The Veterans of Foreign Wars had meeting halls across the country that were rented out for community events.) The Saints were a tight five-piece band with a great singer, and they covered the hits of the day such as The Who's "My Generation' and songs by The Stones and The Yardbirds. They weren't just another garage band. They had professional gear (Fender guitars and amps, and Kustom amps) and great stage presence, and their standard of excellence stuck with me. If you were going to play, then work on it and play well. As importantly, they were local. We figured that if The Saints could be that good, so could we, if we put in the time and had comparable equipment. A nonmusician might not think equipment is such a big deal, but consider what it might be like to climb a steep mountain wearing plastic flip flops or writing a novel on an old typewriter or cooking a five-course meal on a campfire. Yes, the equipment matters, and our equipment was substandard. It was a problem that we needed to fix.

We found a small Bogen p.a. (public address) system to sing through. It came in a suitcase-type of system that folded together so you could carry it with one hand. This unit cost about $50 used and we all chipped in for it. Jim's dad thought the Bogen was a piece of crap, but it's all we could afford, and for a bunch of rookie teenage musicians it seemed pretty fine at the time. Buying the Bogen meant that we no longer had to put vocals through guitar amps, making it possible to set the guitar amps properly. This meant the vocals were clearer and the harmonies sharper. It was one small addition that made a big difference to the quality of our sound.

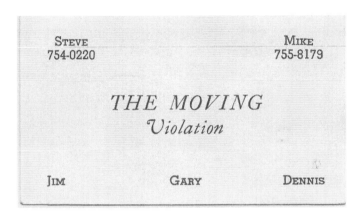

Any book about a band has to deal with the naming of the band. The Rolling Stones picked their name from a Muddy Waters tune, a collective nod of their heads to the Blues that they all loved. Buddy Holly and The Crickets were so dubbed when they were recording a song and discovered a chirping on the song that had been made by a cricket lodged in the walls of the studio. In January of '67, we were all looking for a name. Jim and Gary, who loved to bowl (immensely popular in the Midwest), were bowling at an alley in Park Forest one day when they apparently grew bored. They grabbed a phone book and started leafing through it. Jim stumbled on an ad that used the term 'moving violations' (most likely from a lawyer who offered to defend drivers who had been ticketed for moving violations such as speeding or running a red light.) Jim thought "Moving Violation" made a cool name and so they presented it to the band and we all agreed. If you had too many moving violations, you could lose your drivers license. The name also insinuated somebody being violated, which had naughty undertones. We discussed whether the name should be singular or plural, and decided on singular, though many erroneously called us The Moving Violations. Friends took to calling us the MV5, but we were officially The Moving Violation.

The Chicago Jewish community had been centered on the south side of the city for generations, but as African-Americans started to move in after World War II the Jews headed north of the city to what is referred to as the North Shore, an area that runs north along Lake Michigan from Evanston to Highland Park and on toward Waukegan. Some Jews, however, moved further south. A majority of students at Homewood-Flossmoor were, in fact, Jewish. The reason this mattered to a young Gentile musician like me is that one of the local synagogues developed a reputation for hosting great dances in the 60s. The last time I had been at Temple Anshe Sholom was in eighth grade at a graduation dance that featured my friend Ross' band, The Fugitives. The hall at Temple Anshe Sholom was a good sized room with great acoustics, a big stage and plenty of space for dancing. Although it might have been designed for Jewish holiday celebrations, it was pretty sweet for dances featuring live local bands. In fact, Temple Anshe Sholom was the best local venue at the time, and when we were asked to play there— February 11— it represented our first time on a real stage and first time playing at a dance. By the way, today people go to concerts to hear music. If they dance it is incidental. In the 50s and early 60s young people went primarily to dance. It mattered little whether there was a live band or a record player. It wasn't until the Beatles that dancing faded in importance, replaced by the desire to see a live musical act. The Moving Violation benefitted from this new trend. We were getting paid to play on a real stage, at a popular venue, which inspired us to practice more and take the music even more seriously. Friends who stopped by practice told us that we were getting better and that they dug our sound. This filled us with confidence, which may explain why I wasn't that nervous about playing in public. Even though we had a small p.a. system and mediocre amps, it sounded pretty good in the hall at the temple (the terrific acoustics helped) and the audience was very appreciative.

It was after the Temple Anshe Sholom job that I decided I had to have my own amp, something that would match my aspirations as a musician. I was tired of borrowing one of Jim's amps or plugging into somebody else's amp, which severely limited my ability to adjust my own sound. By this time Jim and his dad had bought a Fender Bandmaster, a really nice amp. It was a Fender—one of the top names in rock music in those days—a piggyback which meant it had a separate power head that sat on top of the speaker cabinet. The cabinet contained two 12-inch speakers that produced a clear sound. And it was loud. It was a top quality amp used by professionals and I was determined to own one.

In March of '67 we didn't have any jobs and for a spell we had fewer practices, though I don't remember why. Spring break was approaching and we planned on spending a lot more time in Mike's basement whipping The Moving

Violation into musical shape. I had a part-time job working for Steve Small's father at his carwash. Since I had my own income to pay for it, my parents gave me permission to order a new amplifier from Reynolds music store. Reynolds was a traditional music store that sold traditional instruments such as pianos, their big seller. It was a proper music store, kind of stuffy, but they were an authorized Fender musical instrument dealer and offered a time payment plan which allowed struggling musicians to pay for their instruments with monthly installments. At the time I was drawn to Reynolds because they were the nearest authorized Fender dealer and I was determined to buy a Fender Bandmaster amp. My parents co-signed, I ordered the amp, and I was sky high with excitement. I was told it would take three weeks to arrive—far too long for an impatient 15 year old—but I was psyched that my first new amp would be such a quality product.

Just before my 16th birthday in April I received a call from Reynolds Music that my amp was in. I was sitting on top of the world, couldn't wait to get it home and plug it in. My mother drove me over to Reynolds and when I saw my amp for the first time, I couldn't believe my eyes. The speaker cabinet was twice as big as I had expected it to be. I wasn't going to complain about the size because I was so excited to finally have the amp, but it took two people to get it into my mom's car and two people to carry it down the stairs to Mike Kennedy's basement. As we carried it down the stairs Jim's eyes opened wide in shock. "They gave you the wrong cabinet," he repeatedly chanted. When we set it down next to Jim's Bandmaster it was immediately apparent how enormous mine was. Jim was convinced that my Fender held two 15-inch speakers—it was definitely big enough for two 15-inchers—yet our inspection revealed two 12-inch speakers, which is what I had expected. This was apparently a new cabinet design, though it was a baffling development. I loved the sound and look, but it would be a bear to drag an amp of that size to shows.

My friend Kurt Rosecrans had a Ford Mustang and we would load my amp into the backseat of his car. The cabinet barely fit through the door and filled the entire backseat. It was impressively huge, and I was proud that it looked so rock and roll. More important, my Danelectro never sounded so good and clean. My confidence took a substantial leap with the Fender Bandmaster towering behind me. Steve Small had also ordered a Fender Bassman from the same store and it arrived shortly after mine. It too had a larger cabinet than expected so that Jim's amp, which had been the largest in the band, now appeared to shrink by comparison. Of course, Jim's amp was the easiest to move from practice to show, but being teenage boys we thought that size mattered. (This was in the days before subcompact cars and mini-components and Virginia Slim cigarettes. Cars were big, skyscrapers were the rage, football and basketball players were huge, even women's beehive hairdos were big. Today you can buy much smaller and lighter amps and speakers—check out the Bose p.a. system or Mark bass amps—that offer far better sound and portability.) Steve's new amp was critical to The Moving Violation's improved sound. The Bassman produced a deep, rich sound that you could actually feel from across the room. I think that Mike's drumming was ratcheted up a notch or two because he could hear and feel Steve's bass. The improved rhythm section was the foundation of The

Moving Violation, just as Charlie Watts and Bill Wyman formed the foundation of the Rolling Stones.

Now that we had professional quality amps for our instruments, we needed a serious upgrade to the p.a. system so that our two vocalists could match the clarity and power of the guitars and bass. The cabinets for our Bogen p.a. were about 2-1/2 feet tall whereas good bands had speaker columns for their p.a.s that were 5 feet or higher. Steve and I had amps that were 4 feet tall. Our piggyback amps were a formidable looking setup that dwarfed the Bogen in terms of power and appearance. I really felt that our sound was progressing and was different than most other groups. Maybe it was my Danelectro 12-string, maybe it was the tight harmonies that Jim and Gary were laying down; whatever the reason for our different and improved sound, it was definitely a good thing. We were also developing a small following, mostly friends of Mike's and Steve's who went to Bloom, and our practices were turning into informal parties. These fans provided constant positive feedback that boosted our confidence enormously. On a personal level, this was a major development in my life. The overweight kid who lacked confidence and was incredibly awkward with girls, who struggled academically, now had a new, improved identity. When I looked in the mirror I saw a guitar player, and in 1967 guitar players were no longer just sidemen, they were the new gunslinger. (Listen to The Eagles' *Desperado* album, which is based on the guitarist-as-gunslinger concept.) Spring of '67 was a huge time for me. I turned 16, passed my driver's license exam, had a new amp and a hot band, and I was beginning to walk the young man's strut.

Steve, Bob, Jim, Mike, Gary, Dennis (Steve's basement)

In 1967 we heard about a battle of the bands that would be held at the American Legion hall in Chicago Heights in May. This battle was a preliminary to a larger battle; the finalists at Chicago Heights would move on to the next level of competition. There was no entry fee, so a slew of bands signed up. We had been practicing for a few months and were gaining confidence, though part of that confidence came from the better quality equipment we'd slowly acquired. Just like in a marriage, this was a honeymoon period for The Moving Violation. Everybody got along, agreed on which songs to play, and showed up at practice with an idea of what needed to be accomplished. These weren't jam sessions where we doodled around and made noise. Before practice Jim, with occasional help from his dad, would work out chords, he and Gary would practice harmonies, and I was pretty serious about working on my guitar parts. Everybody showed up at practice knowing what songs we were going to work on. People often dropped by our practices, so there was a party atmosphere. There were no personality conflicts, nobody complaining about others not being prepared, which is common at practices. That's why we were able to have a 45-song set list after six months together. The result was that we felt good about what we were doing, though we were far from cocky. Bands that had been together for a couple of years, far better bands, would also be competing at the battle.

We played three songs: The Beatles' "Ticket to Ride" and "If I Needed Someone", and the Byrds' "Feel A Whole Lot Better". We weren't very good. As any musician knows who has played in public—and what we didn't know at the time—is that playing in a large venue is incredibly different than playing in a basement. We were used to playing in the confined quarters of Mike's basement, and we had the equipment and our instruments set to get the right sound for that space. We learned the hard way that playing in a large space like the American Legion hall would produce a dramatically different sound. All of a sudden you can't hear the vocals clearly or the bass disappears or the mix is muddy. The hall was dark and there weren't many people as bands showed up to play, then left shortly afterwards. With no audience response (which brings incredible energy to the performers) and poor sound, the result was a dismal, choppy performance, though not the type of complete disaster that can destroy young bands. For one thing, the best band in the area—The New Troys—was in the same battle, as were a few other well-known local bands. We knew we weren't going to blow everybody away; we had only played a few times in public so our expectations weren't that high. In hindsight we were over our heads, but the battle was a learning experience and we never regretted playing there.

The Moving Violation did have some successes that summer. We played an 8th-grade concert showcase in early June at Washington Junior High and the audience loved us. This may not sound like a big deal, high-schoolers playing a middle-school concert, but the memory remains huge in my mind. Washington had a real stage, big time for teenagers who had been mostly playing in basements. We set up on a stage behind the curtains, so that when the curtains were drawn back we were standing in place, just as we'd seen bands do on TV. I suppose the kids had seen the same TV shows—The Beatles and Rolling Stones and The Kinks on *Ed Sullivan* or *Hullabaloo* or *Shindig*—because they knew just what kids are supposed to do when facing a real live rock and roll band: They jumped up and down and screamed. For a teenage rock band to be faced with screaming girls (sure, 8th-graders, but we were only a few years older) was a big deal. Unlike the Battle of the Bands where we played to an empty, dark room that left us flat, at Washington Junior High we felt like a real rock and roll band. I suppose it's kind of like major college basketball programs that schedule early season games against chumps they can thrash. After beating a school 108-44, you feel ready to take on the world. Yes, the audience was mostly 14-year-olds, but they loved us, and their energy and youthful excitement inspired us to get better and reach for new heights. We were introduced as the curtains were being drawn and we started with Buffalo Springfield's protest song "For What It's Worth" and we nailed it. We only played four songs but we played them well and it felt fantastic.

It was the quest to be better that led us to decide to add a third vocalist in order to achieve the three-part harmony sound of The Byrds and Buffalo Springfield. As anybody who has been part of a team knows (sports, business, entertainment) additions don't always mean improvements. The Moving Violation had a dynamic that worked. I think part of it had to do with the fact that Jim and Gary were two years older; they brought some maturity to the group and provided an anchor. There were no personality conflicts and we all got along well. Yet it still seemed like a good idea to add a vocalist. (Jim and I were talking recently and we both wondered why I wasn't called upon to sing harmonies, especially in light of the fact that I've done a lot of singing since. I guess back in '67 I had yet to do any singing and saw myself as a guitar player, so nobody suggested that I give it a try.) Jim and Gary knew of a singer who also had a pair of professional-grade Wilder speaker columns, which happened to be the missing part of our sound system. The tiny Bogen speaker couldn't do the job required of it: project clear vocals at a high volume that could hold up to screaming guitars. Bob Schmit was in the same class at Rich High School as Jim and Gary, though he was an acquaintance, not a friend. Bob was tall with dark hair, a good-looking guy who could only add to The Moving Violation's popularity. Bob drove a Corvette, which meant that he had to make two trips to bring over his tall speakers. We didn't know anything about his vocal abilities, but even if he wasn't a brilliant singer he was welcome in The Moving Violation, as long as we got to use his Wilder speakers. To be honest, I don't remember much about Bob's singing abilities; I do remember that he complained that Gary sang flat. The few times Bob tried to sing lead he sounded like shit. I suppose his harmonies were adequate. In hindsight, Bob didn't belong in The Moving Violation. He wasn't one of us and never fit in. His Wilder speaker columns, though, were high quality and sounded damn good when hooked up to the Bogen system. It's stupid to add somebody because of their equipment, but even then I was a gear-head and was seduced by those tall Wilder speakers.

Bob Schmit did not last long in The Moving Violation. He seemed bored during the one job he played with us (a swimming pool party), at one point leaning on one of his Wilder speakers. He would also ask Gary if he was purposely singing flat. Just as bad, he tried to harmonize every word, rather than be judicious and harmonize at key moments to accent phrases or specific words. Listen to great harmonies by the Byrds or Crosby, Stills and Nash, and you'll notice that sometimes there is a single voice, sometimes two, and occasionally all three singers harmonize. Bob wanted to sing all the time, which doesn't work. Since we liked Gary's vocals and knew that Bob's attempts to sing lead had failed dismally, his jabs at Gary did not go down well. Bob might have been a nice guy, but he was a square peg trying to fit into our round hole. His comments weren't cool, his harmonizing failed, and he had a bad attitude. Jim took to referring to him as a douche. After that first gig with Bob we stopped telling him where or when we were practicing. Eventually we replaced him with Steve Crosse, a guy who used to hang out at our practices and who could really sing.

I couldn't possibly talk about the summer of '67 without mentioning The Beatles' *Sgt Pepper's* album. Prior to *Sgt Pepper's* there was pop, soul, R & B, electric folk and early rock. *Sgt Pepper's* was a game changer. Everybody was excited when any new Beatles album was coming out, but *Sgt Pepper's*, with its arty cover, elicited more excitement than usual. I ran out and bought the album when it first came out, as did my bandmates, and when we first listened to it our musical world changed. It opened the door for psychedelics, for Cream and Jimi Hendrix, it changed the way everybody played and listened to music. Regarding The Moving Violation, one of the first things we did was to learn a song from *Sgt Pepper's*, "With A Little Help From Our Friends". We also adjusted our sound a bit. Paul McCartney's bass was so up front, so strong, that we mixed Steve's bass a bit stronger as well. We also added some choppier strumming, as per "Getting Better All The Time", where the strum is followed by muting by hand. These were small changes, but they reflected a new direction that was driven by *Sgt Pepper's*. The jangly 12-string guitar tunes that were usually about three minutes long soon gave way to distortion and extended jams.

Although Jim and Gary graduated in June from Rich Central, that didn't mean the end of The Moving Violation. Neither went away to college and both were into The Moving Violation and into making it a better band. Great music was coming out of California and traveling across the Atlantic from England, and every musician was inspired. That wave caught The Moving Violation with its full force. A few weeks after the Washington Junior High show we played a party at Skyline Pool, a private swimming club. (Phone numbers in those days started with two letters. Mine was SK5-7839, meaning I lived in the Skyline phone district.) This wasn't a fancy country club with tennis and golf, it was a bare looking swimming pool surrounded by yellow cinderblock and a chain-link fence. The membership fee was inexpensive, making it accessible to most people. We played in the early evening while people swam. We were paid about $60, plus we got to watch girls in bikinis, not a bad summer gig for a teenage band. The downside was that this was the gig where Bob proved once and for all that he didn't belong in The Moving Violation. Besides leaning on his Wilder speakers as if he was tired or too bored to stand up on his own, he also sang with one finger stuck in his ear, something you occasionally see singers do when the music is so loud that it's hard to hear clearly. When Bob stuck his finger in his ear, though, he looked goofy. Maybe Bob was miffed that we hadn't given him any leads to sing. Maybe he realized that he didn't fit in The Moving Violation and was only kept in the lineup for his Wilder speakers. Maybe he liked sticking his finger in his ear.

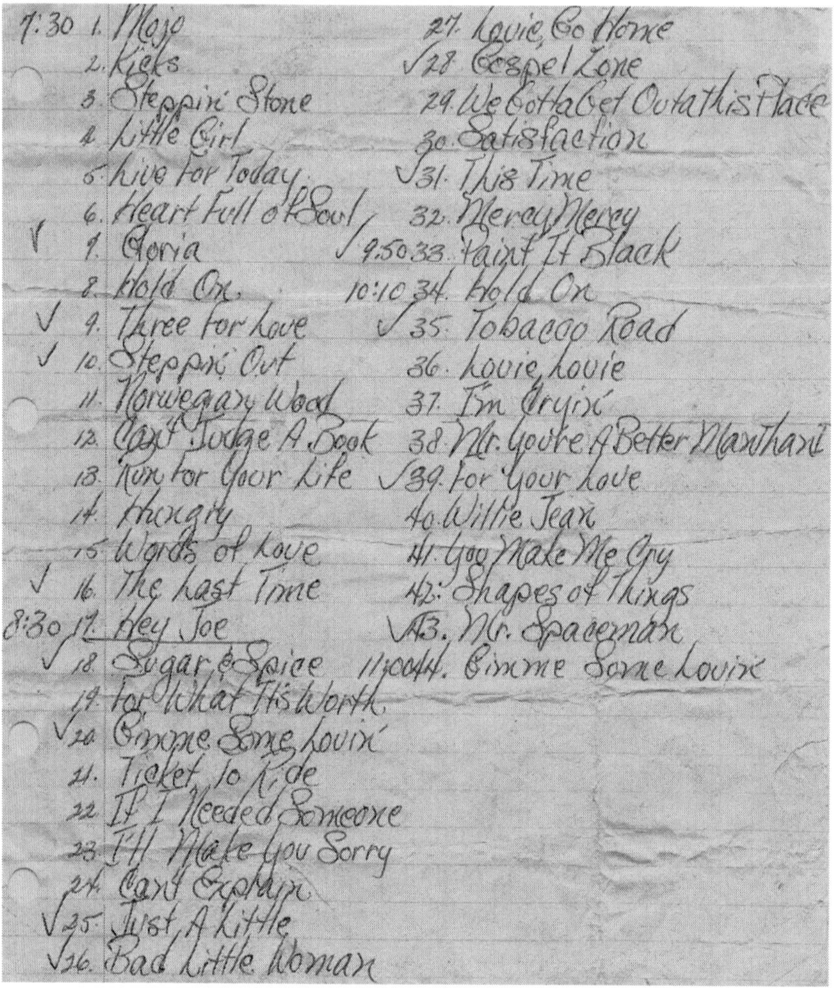

The handwritten set list reads:

7:30
1. Mojo
2. Kicks
3. Steppin' Stone
4. Little Girl
5. Live for Today
6. Heart Full o' Soul
✓ 7. Gloria
8. Hold On
✓ 9. Three for Love
✓ 10. Steppin' Out
11. Norwegian Wood
12. Can't Judge A Book
13. Run for Your Life
14. Hungry
15. Words of Love
✓ 16. The Last Time
8:30 17. Hey Joe
✓ 18. Sugar & Spice
19. For What It's Worth
✓ 20. Gimme Some Lovin'
21. Ticket To Ride
22. If I Needed Someone
23. I'll Make You Sorry
24. Can't Explain
✓ 25. Just A Little
✓ 26. Bad Little Woman

27. Louie, Go Home
✓ 28. Gospel Zone
29. We Gotta Get Outa This Place
30. Satisfaction
✓ 31. This Time
32. Mercy Mercy
9:50 33. Paint It Black
10:10 34. Hold On
✓ 35. Tobacco Road
36. Louie Louie
37. I'm Cryin'
38. Mr. You're A Better Man Than I
✓ 39. For Your Love
40. Willie Jean
41. You Make Me Cry
42. Shapes of Things
✓ 43. Mr. Spaceman
11:00 44. Gimme Some Lovin'

Pool Party Set List

We played three hours and considered it a successful show, though not as thrilling as the one at Washington Junior High. People were swimming and chatting, but many listened to our songs and we also had some friends there who supported us. It was all squeaky clean, with no booze or drugs, typical of the Midwest in '67. It might have been

52

the summer of love in California, with hippies dropping LSD and smoking pot, but it was still pretty square in Chicago, a city dominated by Mayor Daley's Democratic Party machine, trade unions and organized crime. At one point two older guys in suits were standing outside the chain-link fence, checking us out. We thought they might be tough guys from the union or the mob, which was huge in Chicago Heights. (More on that later.) We hadn't joined the union or paid union fees, so a visit from union guys wouldn't have been that unusual. Stories had been circulating about mob guys kicking in amps and drum kits of bands who hesitated to join unions and pay their dues. It added some intrigue to the evening as we knew unions were connected to the mob, and we had a healthy fear of the Chicago mob. This was, after all, the home of Al Capone. It was scary and thrilling and mostly just rumors; it turned out that the two guys outside the fence were scouting us out for a small club that was looking for new bands. In truth, this was a safe suburban experience: no drugs or booze, no gangs or guns, just nice girls and clean-cut guys. Even without gangsters, it was an odd job because of Bob's behavior, though it made it easier for us to drop him from The Moving Violation.

We were still into the harmonies of groups such as The Byrds and Buffalo Springfield, which meant adding another singer, and we were fortunate to be able to add Steve Crosse to The Moving Violation. Steve had gone to elementary school with Steve Small and Mike Kennedy, and often hung out at our practices. More important, he was an accomplished singer, having sung in school choirs since middle school. He had been selected for honor choir, which was limited to about eight of the Bloom High School's

53

eighty or so choir members. Steve was also known for singing along to songs on the radio in Jim Cain's black Ford Falcon. Steve was a little shorter than Jim, had brown hair and brown eyes, wore wire-rim glassed, and went to Bloom High School. He lived with his mother and sister near Bloom, and became the youngest member of the band, being a few months younger than Steve Small and Mike. He was also a bit wilder than the rest of us and the first to dabble in drugs. Drug use was pretty rare at that point and we weren't concerned about the rumors of Steve's drug use, mostly because we really didn't have any idea what it meant. Steve readily admits that he became a fairly serious druggy in high school, starting with pot and working his way to barbiturates and LSD by senior year. We'd all heard stories of pot smoking in California and heard drug lyrics in songs, but it had no meaning to us. Steve had just returned from a trip to Italy with his mother when he sang with us for the first time in August. We were impressed by his ability to 'do parts' as he called it, meaning Steve could sing melody or harmony with confidence. We liked his voice, liked what he added to the vocal mix, and liked him as a person. So Steve Crosse was in and Bob Schmit was out, though we kept his Wilder speakers for a while. Bob eventually lost patience and came over to get his speakers. Of course, since he was driving a Corvette he could fit in only one of the massive speaker columns at a time, so he had to make two trips. I'm sure it pissed him off, but we didn't really care.

Steve Crosse loved being in The Moving Violation. He was a smallish, quiet kid who was virtually invisible in the crowded halls of Bloom. Kids at Bloom now knew Steve as a member of The Moving Violation. What they didn't know is that Steve was one of the hipper kids at Bloom. He started going to concerts with his cousin when he was thirteen, which is about when he started smoking pot. His cousin also turned Steve on to Frank Zappa and other fringe music. Steve would attend the Chicago Democratic Convention of 1968 (infamous for riots, tear gas, demonstrations and mass arrests) and met the poet Allen Ginsburg there. He also regularly hung out on Wells Street in Old Town, attending shows at the Quiet Knight club. He would prove to be a valuable addition to The Moving Violation. Although one of the quieter members—along with me—who had minimal input when it came to song selection, Steve's vocals added a vital element to our sound.

At the time we all knew that Steve Crosse was into drugs, and we thought he was the only stoner in the group. What I didn't know is that Mike Kennedy, a very private person in high school, was also a stoner, though he apparently kept his drug use under the radar. Indeed, Mike was private, but I can't help but feel that I was incredibly naïve. Then again, it was a pretty idyllic time and Mike was never a friend outside of The Moving Violation, unlike Steve Small and, later, Jim Cain.

Summer of '67 brought other changes. My dad and I flew by jet to Connecticut to see relatives, the first time that either of us had flown in a jet, and it was special to share that experience with my dad. I got to hang out with my cousin Ron, who was one year older, and his cool friends. It may not seem like much, but minor episodes in our lives often add up to something bigger. This was one of those episodes. Since New Canaan, Connecticut, was close to New York, we went into the city a few times. We were in the audience for the TV show *To Tell The Truth*, walked

55

through Times Square where I bought some loud flower ties (which I later wore while performing), saw my first panhandler; and, most important, I went to a record store and saw Jimi Hendrix's first album, *Are You Experienced*. We had all heard about Hendrix's amazing performance at the Monterrey Pop Festival and were eager to hear his music. I didn't get to hear the album until I got back to Chicago, but I felt like some hip jetsetter, returning with a Jimi Hendrix album that I had bought in New York City. Today, when people fly to Paris and Bangkok and go on safaris in Africa, a week-long trip to Connecticut and New York doesn't seem like a big deal; in 1967, just before my junior year, it was very exhilarating.

Are You Experienced provided some tangible consequences from my trip, introducing us to new sounds and tunes that would begin to alter The Moving Violation. As happened to so many young musicians (and nonmusicians), *Are You Experienced* blew our minds. The music was silky smooth, yet incredibly powerful and wild, and nobody had ever heard the guitar sounds that Hendrix created. We immediately agreed that we needed to have some fuzz tones, which were essential to the new sound. Most of the popular bands were now employing distortion devices that created new guitar sounds; the 12-string jangle had quickly become old school. Jim and I bought a fuzz tone called a Boss Tone by Jordan, a small 3x3-inch box that was plugged directly into the guitar. Eventually Jim figured how to rewire it and plug it directly into the amp, which worked a lot better. It was a strange little unit that made a big difference to our sound. We dropped some older tunes such as "Gloria" and Paul Revere and the Raiders pop numbers, added the fuzz tone to two guitars,

56

and probably played louder and with more confidence. With the addition of Hendrix's "Purple Haze" and "Foxy Lady" our sound was now heavier—the term used in those days for louder, more intense music; the name Led Zeppelin implies something heavy that soars—and hipper.

Mike Kennedy

By late August, 1967, I was gearing up for the start of my junior year of high school. Jim and Gary were set up with classes at a junior college. With my new found confidence from my trip to the East Coast and our new musical style, I was feeling pretty excited about the new year, socially at least. Shortly after the start of school I met a sophomore by the name of Lee Abrams. Lee was an amazingly energetic young guy who was incredibly passionate about listening to music and making records. Lee remembers hearing Chicago's WLS radio station in 1962 and becoming hooked on radio and music. He subscribed to Billboard and Cashbox, trade magazines about the music industry rather than about musicians. He also listened to Florida radio stations and raved about the music he was hearing. Like so many young men at the time (rock and roll was mostly a male domain) he bought a guitar, but his true interest was the music business, in particular radio and production. Around 1965 people became familiar with Brian Epstein, the Beatles' manager, and it was now more acceptable to be involved in the business end of music. He was so slick and knowledgeable that he could have had his own radio show, but first he wanted to try his hand at producing a record. Lee's first effort was recording a local folk act, The Guy Kranis Trio. Guy Kranis was a senior at Homewood-Flossmoor. The record never went anywhere, nor, apparently, did Guy's musical career. Two months later, Lee was ready to record something other than folk, and he knew that rock and roll was just the thing. The Moving Violation was reaching new creative heights, so we were a natural match. We respected what this eager fifteen-year-old Jewish kid had done musically and, unquestionably, we were awed by his reputation for nasty pranks.

Beware the poor neighbor who pissed off Lee. His most infamous prank—a two-week long series of pranks, in fact—was directly linked to The Moving Violation. Lee tried to sell stock to raise money for the recording at Recordings Unlimited. Lee's neighbor, a geeky kid, reported Lee to the Federal Security and Exchange Commission for selling stock illegally. Lee received a letter from the SEC ordering him to desist selling unauthorized stocks. Lee launched a major campaign to punish the neighbor who was trying to disrupt his business. One day Lee went through the phone book—A to Z—and found anybody who made deliveries: air-conditioning, taxis, pizzas, TV repairs, anybody. Lee asked for deliveries at the same time, then sat in his bedroom and watched as the delivery trucks and cars blocked the street, causing a traffic jam that required police intervention. Since this was before caller IDs, nobody knew who was responsible. Another day Lee ordered magazine subscriptions for dozens of magazines such as Soybean Monthly. The neighbor was flooded with magazines and bills for the magazines. One of the nastier pranks regarded the neighbor's prized shrubs. Lee called a landscaping crew and—posing as the neighbor—told them he wanted to redo his entire yard. The crew showed up next door and pulled out the prized trees and shrubs. This type of mayhem went on for two weeks until the police showed up at Lee's door. He agreed to stop terrorizing the neighbors and they agreed not to bring charges. Stories about Lee's antics slowly leaked out and deservedly earned him a reputation as a mad genius. We figured that anybody with that kind of passion and focus—even if it was used for such nasty business—was a person who could do something for The Moving Violation. We were excited to be associated with Lee.

Guy Kranis was published on Lee Records, but after the Kranis 45 came out, Lee received a legal letter informing him that the name Lee Records was already being used. Thus was born Gem Records, which is on the label of The Moving Violation's 45. Lee's parents were hesitant at first about his new interest, worrying that it would interfere with his school work. (It did, in fact, interfere. Lee never went to college, something frowned upon in the Jewish community to which his family belonged.) His parents became even more concerned when record companies and distributors started to call his house. Some sounded like hoodlums, which a few probably were as the mob had a hand in many Chicago and Midwest businesses. Ultimately, Lee's parents supported his passion, which would become his life's work. The Chicago sound was just emerging in 1965 with local bands such as the Buckinghams and the Shadows of Knight leading the way. Local radio stations were eager to introduce the newest, hottest bands, hoping to discover the new—Chicago—Beatles. Lee wasn't interested in managing bands, finding jobs and such; he was interested in radio, and he thought that finding the next hot band and getting them on the radio could be a way to get his foot in the door.

Lee had seen us play and came to a practice in Mike Kennedy's basement for a closer look. He apparently liked what he saw—and heard—and decided that we were the right band for him to make a record with. In spite of his age, we were flattered. He talked a good game and we thought the whole thing was unbelievable. "Are you really going to record us, in a recording studio?" and Lee assured us that was his plan. He set us up in mid-September to go to Recordings Unlimited, a downtown Chicago studio at 64 Van Buren Street. Lee did his research in Billboard, which had an annual issue that listed studios. He called around and learned that the big studios charged up to $125 an hour. He chose Recordings Unlimited because it charged a mere $25 per hour with a three hour minimum. The studio owner, Oren Stembel, doubled as recording engineer; he said he enjoyed recording young people. Oren Stembel wore a bow tie, not the hippest look, but his equipment and studio were adequate and he seemed to know what he was doing. Some of the regional Battle of the Bands included a recording session at Recordings Unlimited among the winner's prizes. The studio was probably a three-track affair, pretty low tech, but it was the real deal with a soundboard that allowed the engineer to adjust sound levels to achieve the best sound possible. (Recording studios would soon feature eight- and sixteen-track recordings which would allow all sorts of sound magic.)

WA 2-2340

OREN STEMBEL

recordings unlimited

Recording Studio: 64 E. Van Buren - Chicago; Illinois

The recording session took place on a Saturday. The A side of the 45 was "This Time", music by Jim Cain, lyrics by Gary Harn. "This Time" was a gentle pop tune similar to the Association's "Cherish", a blatant attempt at producing a commercial hit. Although we were getting into Jimi Hendrix, we apparently were still willing to do a pop tune in our quest for success. After all, "Cherish" was all over the radio whereas you could only hear Hendrix on home stereos or played by live bands in clubs. Like The Association, The Byrds and Beach Boys, we were going for a tight harmony sound at that time. The recent addition of Steve Crosse made it possible for The Moving Violation to approach that vocal quality, as can be heard on the 45. The B side was "Three For Love", written by Joe Kelly, a member of the Shadows of Knight, one of the Chicago area's most popular bands. "Three For Love" featured a 12-string guitar, probably one of the reasons why we selected it.

Lee, Steve C, Jim, Gary, Dennis, Mike, Steve S

The studio had microphones but we had to drag all of our amps, Mike's drum kit, and other equipment to the recording studio in a station wagon and one other car. It was urban, so we had to cram everything into an elevator and lug it into the studio. Recordings Unlimited was a single-room studio, not impressive by future standards, but it was nirvana to us. I mean, we were in a real studio and we heard our recordings played back to us, the first time we had actually heard ourselves. This was not playing at a pool to a bunch of kids in swim suits; this was recording in a real studio with a live engineer. Far out! I don't remember any details. We didn't take a lot of time, didn't dub vocals or do any fancy effects. I do remember that Lee was a bit anxious, possibly because he was paying by the hour, though more likely because Lee was emotionally invested in the recording and wanted it to work. Lee was not some amateur music fan who wanted to record for fun; at the age of 15 he was already focusing on radio broadcasting and music promotion as a career. So when we heard a popping sound on one of the playbacks, Lee was concerned. It turned out that the noise came from the pop machine in the hallway whenever anybody dropped in their quarter to get a Coke. Lee rolled his eyes and pulled his hair, and made sure the machine was unplugged before we continued. We recorded two songs and got out of there. It was, after all, Lee's money and he was paying by the clock. We spent about three hours at Recordings Unlimited, a small studio used mostly for demos rather than the production of entire albums, but it was big-time for The Moving Violation.

Jim Cain believes that Oren Stembel seemed to be taking his time, perhaps in an effort to squeeze a few more dollars out of Lee. Stembel kept messing with the drum sound, adding reverb effects that muddied the sound. He also claimed to need to answer the phone, even though the phone wasn't ringing. Jim and Gary joked about Stembel dragging the session to pad the bill. Of course, that was Lee's concern, not the band's. As Jim recently said, "Look, I'd been playing guitar for about a year and I'm in a recording studio. I'm just living the dream." The master tape had to be sent to Kelmar Studio in Cleveland (inexpensive, also discovered in Billboard) and we waited for over a month before the 45s arrived. I can't express how amazing it was to finally hold our record, another of life's highlights.

The 45 was sent around to radio stations and got some air play in Chicago Heights and Hammond, Indiana, though never on the big Chicago stations like WCFL or WLS. It never caught on. Lee thinks that The Moving Violation were caught between eras, in his own words, "between the Shadows of Knight era and the Doors". He believes that had it been six months later, and if we had started smoking pot and listening to heavy music sooner, we would have recorded different music. I completely agree with Lee. We were aiming at kids who listened to The Association, but their time was rapidly coming to an end. Within months we would be playing Jimi Hendrix and going for a heavier, more psychedelic sound. Would things have been different if we had recorded a year later? We'll never know. What I do know is that The Moving Violation was heavier than the Guy Kranis Trio, so Lee was moving in the right direction.

Although the 45 had limited circulation and never made any money, it was very important for the band. Unlike today where anybody can record themselves—with impressive results thanks to the incredible software that exists, as well as the quality of recording equipment—recording songs in those days was uncommon and a big deal. It was a huge ego-boost to 'have a 45'; it felt empowering to be able to sell 45s after playing at a dance or a battle of the bands. We all felt cool, though the recording did offer an early hint of a problem that was slowly emerging.

Jim Cain had called Steve Small, really psyched about the 45 and its potential. If the 45 could get radio play, and if people liked it, and if it went national...that sort of dreaming that can be so exhilarating. Apparently, Steve was more of a realist and not that excited. He said that the recording quality was inferior to that of records on the radio, and he told Jim he was being naïve to think the 45 would lead to anything. This really annoyed Jim, in large part because he didn't know what the word naïve meant, though he did understand that it was not a compliment. Jim was put off by Small's lack of enthusiasm, and the disaffection with Small would slowly grow over time.

The 45 was issued by Gem Records—founded and owned by Lee Abrams—in late October. Lee had maybe a few hundred singles pressed and he went around to radio stations to try to get some air time for the record. He also managed some impressive publicity. Old Chicagoans will be familiar with Kup's Column, a daily column in the Chicago Sun-Times written by Irv Kupcinet that focused on society news. Irv Kupcinet was a Chicago personality who also had a TV talk program. People scanned Kup's Column for familiar names, to see where Frank Sinatra had dinner the previous night or to learn which famous Chicagoan was getting married to whom. Kup's Column was eventually syndicated in 100 newspapers and his TV talk show earned fifteen Emmy awards. Lee sent a letter about The Moving Violation and Gem records to Kupcinet at the Chicago Tribune, and received a call from one of Kup's people. They talked with Lee for about an hour and asked if they could send a photographer down to Chicago Heights. Lee eagerly said yes, which led to a mention in the column that blew us away:

Kup got the name of the second song wrong, using the name of the band instead, but it was still amazingly awesome to be mentioned in Kup's Column. Lee was responsible for our mention by Kup and the recording session, and it was obvious that this energetic 15-year-old had a bright future. Those who followed Lee's career know that he fulfilled his promise. Google his name and check out his entry in Wikipedia. Although The Moving Violation didn't play a role in Lee's successful career in the music business, his role as producer of our CD was one of the highlights of our brief existence, topped only by the Bloom Battle of the Bands.

[TRIBUNE Staff Photo]

BUSINESS MAN—Lee Abrams, 15-year-old president and owner of Gem Records, does his office work in his home, 2038 Vardon lane, Flossmoor. Lee founded the company last March and has released one record, by the Moving Violation.

There was a down side, of sorts, to our steadily increasing fame: The musicians' union came knocking at our proverbial door. Chicago is, and has been for a long time, a union town. There is very little economic activity that isn't regulated by unions, from trucking to restaurant workers to musicians. Everybody in Chicago is aware of this, especially around election time when groups such as the Teamsters Union and American Federation of Labor and Congress of Industrial Workers—AFL-CIO—galvanize their members to vote, almost always Democratic. It was also common knowledge that many unions were controlled by the Chicago mob, a very serious criminal organization that you did not want to cross. As musicians, we had heard stories of what happened when musicians failed to pay their dues. According to rumors (we didn't actually know anybody who had been squeezed by unions), instruments and equipment by those who were bold enough—or stupid enough—to defy the union were damaged or destroyed. We were neither bold nor stupid, and we were passionate about our equipment, so when Dennis Montella (Mike Kennedy's brother-in-law) confirmed that we needed to pay our union dues, we went to Lee Abrams for help. Joining the union cost $45 per musician (vocalists didn't have to pay since they didn't play an instrument) plus annual dues. That was a lot of money for high-schoolers in 1967, especially after buying our instruments and amps, and considering we were only earning about $100 per show. Lee talked with his dad, who agreed to loan us the money to join the Chicago Heights Musicians Union, which we did on October 2.

Another side note is in order: Recently I did some research and discovered that Co-op Music, a record store

I used to frequent in Chicago Heights, was investigated for ties to the mob in the 60s, and was suspected of being a business that was set up to launder mob money. Co-op Music was also involved with the jukebox business, which was known to be controlled by the mob. The office of the Chicago Heights Musicians Union happened to be on the second floor of the same building, right above Co-op Music. The mob tie to Co-op is mostly speculation, yet it still gives me a chill to consider how close we might have been to organized crime, which was rampant in Chicago.

Gary Harn

THE CHICAGO HEIGHTS JAYCEES
★ ★ PRESENTS ★ ★
BATTLE OF BANDS
BLOOM FOOTBALL FIELD
10th & CHICAGO ROAD - CHICAGO HEIGHTS, ILL.
IN PERSON
★ ★ IN CONCERT ★ ★
THE FLOCK ▬ THE M. H. ROYALS
★ ★ ALSO ★ ★
THE DUTCH MASTERS
SPONSORED BY ROBERTO'S MUSIC SALON
——CONTENDERS FOR CROWN——
EBBTIDES - REGALS - CHOZEN FEW
JAY WALKERS - NEW CREATION - DRAKES
BAD HABITS - SHALIMARS - REFLECTIONS
CAPT. ZERO & HIS BUSHMEN - SQUIRES
MOVING VIOLATION - POOR BOYS
SUN. - OCT. 15
1:00 P.M. TO 5:00 P.M.
ADMISSION $1.75 AT THE GATE
TICKETS PURCHASED IN ADVANCE $1.50
PURCHASE TICKETS AT B-G MEN'S WEAR, CHICAGO HEIGHTS, ILL.

We didn't have many jobs in summer of '67. There weren't that many live music venues and no school events (kickoff, homecoming, prom), but we continued to practice regularly in Mike's basement, usually Friday night or Saturday afternoon. Friday was the main practice time because Mike's mom Audrey was single and often went out on dates on Friday night. Mike would have his girlfriend over and other people would stop by, so it was always a combination practice and social event. The band members continued to be friends, though the glimmer of our first conflict was starting to emerge. Whereas most of us were devoted to The Moving Violation, Steve Small had other interests, sports in particular. He was a serious runner, and cross country was an autumn sport. That meant that races were usually run on Saturday, which led to inevitable scheduling conflicts. This didn't prove to be a major problem at the time, but after the Bloom Battle of the Bands Steve's priorities and other interests became a serious source of dissension. In late September, though, we were riding high on the session at Recordings Unlimited, eagerly awaiting the release of our single, and we were preparing for the Battle of the Bands.

Battles of the bands were usually sponsored by local businesses as well as regional outfits. One of the sponsors of the battle we entered was B & Gs Men's Wear on Halsted Street, which happened to be where Mike Kennedy's brother-in-law, Dennis Montella, worked. Another sponsor was the Chicago Heights Jaycees, of which Mike's brother-in-law was a member. (This would lead some to claim nepotism when the battle's results were announced.) Other sponsors included Roberto's Music

Salon, (where I bought my first guitar), State Farm Insurance, Fast Printing, and Liberty Lithographers. The battle was originally supposed to be held at Bloom High School on the football field. Three professional Chicago area bands would play short sets: one before the actual battle, one in the middle and one at the end. The most notable of these bands was The Flock, a jazz-rock group which featured Jerry Goodman on violin. Goodman would go on to play with The Mahavishu Orchestra, a group led by guitarist John McLaughlin that achieved a modest level of fame in the early 70s. (McLaughlin and drummer Billy Cobham had played with Miles Davis, which brought instant credibility to the Orchestra. Incidentally, Goodman did not perform at the Bloom battle.) The bands that participated in the battle covered a range of styles: a couple of African-American bands including the Jay Walkers, a band of greasers, popsters, and rock-and-rollers. (By the way, Greasers did not refer to Mexicans, as it did later, but to guys who greased back their hair with products such as Brylcreem. Greasers were tough guys who rolled up cigarette packs in the sleeves of their white T-shirts, wore tight jeans, picked fights and drove fast cars. Many were Italian, but it had more to do attitude than ethnic heritage. They were at the opposite end of the social scene from the hippies who were just emerging. The best known example would be found in the musical *Grease*.) One band, Captain Zero and His Bushman, included Greg Stone, the friend with whom I discovered music, and Ross Barnard, the cool guy who was the first musician I wished to emulate. Ross was Captain Zero.

The weather was nasty the day of the battle, a rainy, grey Chicago day, so the battle was moved from Bloom's football field to the gym. Rather than waste time waiting for each band to set up, a band was set up in each corner of the gym. That meant that there was no delay between bands: when one finished, another set up while the music continued in a different corner of the gym. It was an efficient way to run the event and it kept the music flowing. In addition, there was a main stage set up in the middle of the gym. According to an article in the *Chicago Heights Star* newspaper, nearly 2,000 people showed up for the battle. Although I think the number is inflated, there was still an impressive turnout. As well as band members, family, friends and fans of each band, there were also other musicians and people from the area who were interested in the music. Everybody had seen rock and roll on TV—the *Ed Sullivan show*, *Hullabaloo*, *Bandstand*, *Shindig*, *The Monkees*—but live rock and roll was still relatively new and an ever bigger draw. The audience was mostly white, mostly middle class, yet it represented a wide range of age groups since younger siblings and parents attended. There was no light show (that was happening at the Fillmore East with the Joshua Light Show, a psychedelic experience created by Joshua White), no booze or drugs. It spite of rock and roll's growing reputation for drugs, sex and excess, the Bloom Battle of the Bands was a wholesome affair fit for the entire family. Entry was $1.75, a fairly significant amount in 1967, though apparently not so high as to scare away too many people.

This was a transitional time in American social and musical history. Just as the greasers were slowly disappearing, being replaced by long-hairs, so too was music changing, as well as the fashions sported by the bands. In hindsight, it is apparent that we were caught up in that change, sometimes with one foot in the past and the other striding into the future. That may explain why we were playing "Purple Haze" (the future of rock music) yet decided to wear uniforms for the battle, a decidedly early 60s musical fashion feature. Check out photos of the early Beatles or Beach Boys or dozens of other groups and you'll notice they are wearing matching suits or sweaters or Oxford shirts and tan slacks. Even their haircuts matched. Our early heroes, Paul Revere and The Raiders, wore American Revolutionary War uniforms. The Moving Violation went to a store in Old Town (a hip Chicago neighborhood on the north side) that sold cool clothes such as old military uniforms. (Sgt Peppers.) We all bought white navy cadet jackets that became the uniform of The Moving Violation and became known to some as The Moving Violation coat.

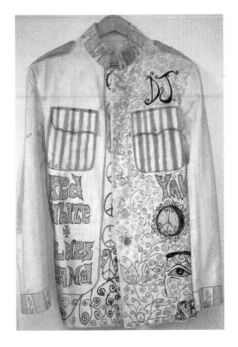

Two of our friends bought the same coats and would wear them to our shows. My mother, who had been in the navy, sewed her naval buttons onto my coat. Mine was eventually painted with funky, colorful designs by Kris Orenberg, a cute, arty girl whose company I enjoyed. Although our pants weren't matching, we all wore dark trousers. Captain Zero and His Bushmen wore military coats as well, theirs featuring epaulets.

Show to Feature 'Battle of Bands', Top Pops Units

Three nationally-known pops groups will head the bill at a Chicago Heights Jaycee-sponsored concert October 15, followed by a "Battle of the Bands" between south suburban combos.

"The Flock," the "MH Royals" and the "Dutchmasters" have performed throughout the country, according to Dennis Montella, chairman of the event, and will lead off the concert scheduled for 1 to 5 p.m. at the Bloom high school football field.

A total of $500 in cash prizes, and a plaque proclaiming "Champion Band of the Area," will be awarded to winners in the musical competition.

* * *

AMONG the contestants will be "The Regals," "The Bad Habits," "The Drakes," "The Squires," "The Shalimars," "Capt. Zero and His Bushmen," "The New Creation," "The Moving Violation," "The Poor Boys," "The Jay Walkers," "The Reflections" and "The Chosen Few."

Tickets, at the advanced sale price of $1.50, may be obtained from members of the competing bands. Tickets, at $1.75, may also be purchased at the gate.

"This event is primarily for the young people of the area and is designed to give participants valuable experience, recognition and the opportunity to associate with top name bands," said Chicago Heights Jaycee president James Sheehan.

Chicago Heights Star Newspaper

We were allowed fifteen minutes for the battle, which means 3-4 songs. We chose the soul number "Knock On Wood"; the Beatles' "With A Little Help From My Friends", one of our best tunes; and "Purple Haze". We didn't play either of the songs from our 45 because we wanted popular tunes that would galvanize the audience. Slow love songs and pop tunes were rejected. A large cheering section showed up, including a bunch of freshmen girls who were dropped off by their parents. (Steve Crosse remembers dating a few of those freshman, a side benefit of being in The Moving Violation.) Lee had urged us to pack the battle with our fans and supporters, so Lee and I went to the library during our free periods (I didn't waste too much of my school time actually studying) and chatted up freshmen girls, encouraging them to show up for the battle. Everybody had seen the Beatles and Stones on TV, and had witnessed hordes of girls going berserk. That's what we were hoping for, and that's what we got. Our cheering section went wild when we played, which may have beneficially influenced the judges. To be fair, I have to give most of the credit to Lee. He wasn't in it for the money; Lee was driven to make a career in the music industry, which he did. He didn't try to influence our song selection or personnel or playing style; it was the business end, the recording and promotion, that gave him a thrill. Lee Abrams was an innovator who would later be credited with creating the album oriented rock format—AOR—that transformed FM radio. We also liked hanging out with Lee; he was a fun guy who brought great energy.

Not only did we wear uniforms—which was about to become seriously uncool in rock and roll—we also arranged synchronized moves for Purple Haze. Although choreographed dance moves was not a pop thing, it was a standard part of Motown. Chicago has, of course, a huge African-American population and the entire city—black and white—was very much into Motown and soul: The Four Tops, The Temptations, The Supremes, The Jackson Five, James Brown. All these groups used synchronized dance steps and it must have rubbed off on us. Purple Haze was our big number and we started the song with everybody kneeling on their right knee; the three guitar players in front of Mike's drums, the two singers in the front line. As the song starts with its familiar guitar riff, each guitar player jumped to his feet, one at a time, followed by the singers, also one at a time. We also employed some funky moves, including one where the two singers shuffled to their right while the three guitarists shuffled in unison to their left. Pretty cool.

The other bands were a mixed bag. As mentioned previously, the Jay Walkers were African-American who played soul. The Drakes were greasers, mostly Italian guys who slicked their hair back and played "Last Kiss" by J Frank Wilson, a weepy song about a kid killed in a car crash. The song was driven by a Farfisa organ, a very popular instrument at the time, but extremely cheesy in our opinion since we were a guitar-driven band. The Drakes included a couple of instructors from Roberto's Music Salon, so we viewed them as tough competition. Captain Zero and His Bushmen— dressed in flashy uniforms that were much newer and nicer than our second-hand military castoffs—supposedly played rock, though they opened with a pop tune. The Squires were—to be brutally honest—not very good. They knew how to play but weren't that talented and apparently had not put in that much practice time. I don't remember the order, though The Moving Violation were one of the last bands.

Our equipment was out in the hallway. With four stages, and each band playing about 15 minutes, we had plenty of time to set up. (Steve Crosse remembers two stages, not four. Either way, there was a smooth, quick transition between bands.) When one band finished, another band was ready to play while the first band's stage was emptied, then set up for the next group. Bands had to bring everything: drum kit, amps, p.a., mics and mic stands, instruments. The Moving Violation were very relaxed while we waited, just hanging out and listening to the earlier bands. We thought we were pretty cool and nobody exhibited any signs of nerves. We were focused on playing. When the time came we carried our equipment to the stage we'd been assigned and set up as usual. The two vocalists—Steve Crosse and Gary Harn—were in front. The two guitarists and bassist—Jim Cain, me and Steve Small —were in the middle row. Mike Kennedy, his drum set, and the amps were in the back row. When we were announced we took the stage with the confidence that is so common among teenage boys who have adrenaline coursing through their veins. Our first song, Eddie Floyd's "Knock on Wood", went down well with the crowd that was familiar with the soul tune. "With A Little Help From My Friends" was a straight cover that was also well received. We nailed "Purple Haze" and were rewarded by the audience with cheers and shouts. When you're into playing, you're not aware of details such as who is screaming and who is dancing. What you feel is the energy, and the Bloom gym buzzed with great, happy energy. We didn't know if we had delivered a winning set, but we knew we had played better than ever before and we knew that the crowd loved our performance.

When the winners were announced, our feeling that we had played well was confirmed. The Moving Violation was named co-winners with The Drakes. The two bands split the 1st and 2nd place prize money, with each band walking off with $175 and a mountain of pride. Some sore losers claimed that the results were fixed, especially since The Drakes included music instructors from Roberto's Music Salon, one of the sponsors of the battle. The Moving Violation, on the other hand, had no direct connections to sponsors or judges (other than Mike's brother-in-law

Dennis Montella). At the time I believed that The Drakes would have been named sole winner (they were really good, not a surprise since they featured professional musicians) but the charges of a fix would have been too strong. I believe we won because the judges liked what we did. Instead of some weepy love song driven by Farfisa organ, the judges saw versatility (blue-eyed soul, the latest in psychedelia, pop Beatles) and showmanship (uniforms and dance steps). "Purple Haze" had only come out a few months earlier, so we were current. Maybe we were selected as co-winners to make it look more legitimate, but with the possible exception of The Drakes, we were the best band that day.

Jim still fondly remembers the battle. His dad was there to see The Moving Violation win, and members of other bands stopped by to offer praise. Jim was leaning on a speaker, his shirt partially unbuttoned to show some chest, and he was feeling pretty cool. Suddenly, a girl of about six walked over carrying a piece of paper and asked for his autograph. His sense of cool evaporated and he was left feeling embarrassed. If some high school hottie had asked for his phone number it would have been different, but a six-year-old autograph seeker put things in perspective.

The next day I awoke feeling something I had not felt in a long time, if ever: I felt like going to school! Wow, did we really win the Chicago Heights Battle of the Bands? Maybe I would finally be somebody, a guitar stud, a musical hero. My excitement quickly faded when I arrived at school to discover that I was not suddenly 'cool' just because we'd won the battle. In fact, the victory had turned me into a villain, and I was more unhappy than ever to be a student at Homewood-Flossmoor rather than Bloom. Captain Zero and His Bushmen were from H-F and they were, in Lee Abram's words, "pissed" about losing to The Moving Violation. Steve Crosse said that it was a great day for him at Bloom. He was recognized and greeted by people who hadn't known him previously. All of a sudden he was somebody. Those of us from The Moving Violation who attended H-F had a very different experience. Lee Abrams was hassled after the battle by some of the Bushmen. Greg Stone confronted Lee with, "How could you do this to me? I thought we were friends." Steve Paul, another of the Bushmen, told Lee that he better not show his face. (Steve Paul was a little guy, not much of a threat to Lee.) Our two fans who had purchased The Moving Violation military jackets walked into Stone's Hobby Shop wearing the coats, and they were supposedly chased out by the very emotional Mrs. Stone who felt that we had unfairly won. I was particularly hurt by this hostility because just three years earlier I was good friends with Ross Barnard (Captain Zero himself) and Greg Stone. It was, of course, teen hostility and jealousy, and nobody was in any real danger. We won fairly—in my opinion—but the next day I was once again just another student at Homewood-Flossmoor, a school at which I never felt I belonged. I could share my excitement with Lee and some of the girls who showed up at the battle, but otherwise I kept a low profile.

For most of us in The Moving Violation, the battle at Bloom was a high point of our young lives. Many young men will point to losing their virginity as the outstanding moment of their youth. For me, winning the battle was one of the highlights of my teen years. This was a transitional time in American society. Until the mid-sixties, the big men on campus (BMOCs) were jocks. Now, with the Beatles and Rolling Stones on TV and all the 'hip' shows like *Shindig* and *The Monkees*, musicians were becoming cool. Being a member of a well known band, one that had won a highly publicized battle of the bands, meant guys with long hair could now be BMOCs, at least to some portions of the student body. With a 45 and first place in the Bloom battle, we had gone from invisible students to minor stars. Life was good.

A CHICAGO HEIGHTS JAYCEES PRODUCTION

Battle of Bands

PARTICIPATING SPONSORS

B-G Men's Wear
Liberty Lithographers
Chicago Heights Block

State Farm Ins. Co.
Fast Printing
Joyce Trucking

Roberto's Music Salon

IN CONCERT

THE FLOCK & THE M.H. ROYALS
ALSO
THE DUTCHMASTERS

CONTENDERS for CROWN

The Moving Violation
Capt. Zero and His Bushmen
The Shalmars
The Reflections
The New Creation
The Regals

The Poor Boys
The Squires
The Bad Habits
The Drakes
The Jay Walkers
The Chozen Few

The Ebb Tides

CHAPTER SEVEN - WHAT GOES UP MUST COME DOWN

Bloom High School Blue and White Dance (February '68)

Some things changed with the victory at the battle of the bands, though not all for the better. We started landing more jobs, which meant more money. For the next few months we had 2-3 paying jobs per month and our record was getting air play on a few Chicago area radio stations such as WRHS, WIND, WLTH AND WJOB, all minor local stations. Lee also sold our records at our shows for around 50 cents each, though we never saw any of that money since it paid for the recording session. We were making peanuts, yet it felt special at the time. Remember, we only had half a dozen jobs in about a year prior to the battle, so winning the battle and landing all these jobs was a huge leap and very exciting. Getting rich wasn't as much a goal as becoming famous. What I didn't know at the time is that while Lee Abrams' star was rising, the days of The Moving Violation were winding down. Sadly, our last show with the original lineup was at Bloom's Blue and White dance. The Blue and White dance was the culmination of a week's activities designed to celebrate school spirit. (Bloom's colors were blue and white, of course.)

SET 1

1. Hold On	21. Purple Haze
2. Mojo	22. Feel A Whole Lot Better
3. Louie Go Home	23. Tree(sure)for Love
4. Ticket To Ride	24. Hey Joe
5. Ben Franklin's Almanac	25. This Time
6. Sugar & Spice	26. Kicks
7. Paint It Black	27. Mr. Spaceman
8. I'll Make You Sorry	28. People Are Strange(reques
9. White Rabbit	29. I'm A Man
10. Mercy,Mercy	30. For Your Love
11. Bad Little Woman	31. You Wouldn't Listen
12. A Little Help	32. If I Needed Someone
13. Born In Chicago	33. Gospel Zone
14. Mr. You're A Better Man	34. Can't Explain
15. Words Of Love	35. Just A Little
16. Gimme Some Lovin	36. Gloria(Request)
17. Make Me Fell So Good	37. Knock On Wood
18. Judge A Book	
19. We Gotta Get Out	
20. Tobacco Road	

Set List for Blue and White Dance

The Saints, a band we looked up to, had played the 1967 Blue and White dance while The Moving Violation were playing at Anshe Sholom temple. Our selection as the band for the 1968 Blue and White dance illustrates how far we had come in one year. We would, however, go no further with the original six.

I suppose that our success led directly to our downfall. Most of us were giddy with excitement over our victory and envisioned a brilliant future of fame and fortune, or at least more success with girls. For some of us, music and The Moving Violation was the most important thing happening in our lives. That wasn't the case for Steve Small. He loved music, but he was not a natural musician and was never as good playing bass as he was at running. Steve loved cross country and track, and he saw music as a fun—though very temporary—hobby. (Steve was accepted to Brown due to grades, great ACT scores, and his record as a runner, and he remains a serious runner to this day.) When he voiced this view to Jim Cain it didn't go down well. As Jim recently pointed out, the band was not part of Steve's dream; it was for the other band members. When Steve expressed skepticism about the band's future—as he had about the 45's success—Jim mentioned it to me and I probably mentioned it to other bandmates and it was agreed that Steve lacked the passion that we expected from every member of band. He had also scoffed at our concerns about the union possibly breaking our equipment, something the rest of us took seriously. In addition, there was some tension between Steve and Mike regarding Mike's girlfriend Cynci, short for Cynthia. At one point Steve called Cynci a Pollyanna (from a book and popular Disney movie of the day, an insulting term for being

86

absurdly optimistic and good-hearted), which infuriated Mike. Another point, one that is vividly remembered today by Steve Crosse, is that Steve Small was highly animated on stage, executing herky-jerky moves and constantly flopping his Beatles haircut. Whereas some might have found this engaging, many in the band and audience saw this as uncool. It is an incredibly ironic that of the six members of The Moving Violation, Steve Small had the most professional success as a musician in later years than any of us, perhaps with the exception of me. I've played music almost nonstop since picking up the Danelectro, but I've never had a hit record in Germany, which Steve did.

To this day Steve feels badly about one incident. During a practice in Mike's basement there was grumbling about the bottom line—the rhythm section—being off. Gary, who was usually a peacemaker, complained that Mike was dragging the pace. Steve, who was never confident about his bass playing, could have spoken up in Mike's defense, but he kept his head down and remained silent. Apparently infuriated by the lack of support, Mike Kennedy stood up, walked behind Steve, and hit him on the head with a drum stick. Steve wasn't so much upset about being whacked by Mike as he was at having failed to defend Mike.

Things turned nasty between Jim and Steve. Jim's girlfriend at the time was a cute greaser named Cindy. Some of the band members told Jim that Steve had been making fun of Cindy and calling her "greaser girl". Jim later discovered that it was Mike Kennedy who was calling Cindy names, but Mike liked to give Steve grief (for fun? a hostile act?). At the time, though Jim believed that Steve was the culprit, probably because he had been upset with

Steve about his attitude toward the 45 and other transgressions. At another time, while sitting in Mike's bedroom, Steve made the comment about Cynci, Mike's girlfriend, being a Pollyanna. Mike leaped across the room, grabbed Steve and slammed him against the wall. When Mike let go, Jim remembers seeing Steve smirk, as if he was pleased to have pushed Mike's buttons so effectively. This didn't sit well with Jim. When the band showed up for practice at Mike's one day, he was geared up for combat. When Steve walked in Jim jumped up, grabbed him by the shirt and started shouting about Steve calling Cindy a greaser girl. Steve was shocked and stumbled backward. To this day Jim is mortified by his actions. He claims that it went against his character and he never—before or since—attacked anybody. Although he didn't actually punch Steve, Jim felt that, in his own words, he "acted like an asshole."

I don't remember anybody actually kicking Steve out of the band, but things became uncomfortable and he apparently decided he had better things to do than come to practice and deal with our bad vibes. Jim remembers that everybody was upset with Steve's attitude and had been giving him grief for various offenses, which would explain why Steve quit. Steve remembers things differently. He remembers clearly that he was fired, though he doesn't remember who delivered the news. To add insult to injury, Steve's bass amp remained with the band, and the amp took the brunt of the band's ire. The remaining band members took off the back of the amp and wrote nasty, juvenile insults on the inner cover. Two years later Steve opened the back and found the insults, including Chink. Although he carries no bad feelings, he does feel that Jim was primarily responsible for his being fired. He was asked to join other bands, but instead focused his energies on academics and running. Steve Crosse traded in his coronet (which he played in middle school band) for a bass, though he never did master it during his time in The Moving Violation. It is not easy to sing and try to maintain a steady rhythm.

It's ironic that, just as the band was falling apart, positive things were occurring for The Moving Violation in terms of public relations. The 45 came out in November, which led to new publicity. An article from December, 1967, in *Bloom Broadkaster*, the Bloom High School newspaper, discussed the recording session and quoted drummer Mike Kennedy, "With moderate success of **Three For Love** we should be going to Universal Studios in Chicago middle of December. Both sides will probably be written by Gary and Jim, and with the better studios and RCA printing, we hope for a real good cut next time around." That recording session never took place.

Mike Kennedy's days in The Moving Violation were also numbered. Jim was never particularly fond of Mike and didn't like the way he treated his girlfriend Cynci, though it wasn't Jim who booted Mike from the band. I have to admit that I'm very embarrassed with my role in his departure. It's an old story (check out George Harrison and Eric Clapton regarding Patty Harrison and "Layla"), but the root of the problem may have been my crush on Cynci. Some of us felt that Mike didn't treat Cynci very well, and the truth is that I felt she deserved better treatment. In an incident that still haunts me to this day, I heard that Mike was screwing another girl while dating Cynci. I called her and ratted out Mike. She called him at work and cried on the phone. (Mike was silk screening for Popeil Brothers, who were famous for selling ultra cheap kitchen devices in late night TV ads.) After work, an enraged Mike drove like a madman to my house, chased by a neighbor who was furious that Mike had driven over his driveway. He drove through a bank's parking lot at about 70 miles an hour. Mike tried to get into my house to administer a beating, but my mom wouldn't let him in. We soon got over that incident, but never fully recovered.

In hindsight, it was typical high school bullshit, featuring doses of jealousy and teen lust. Mike recently said he was not screwing the girl in question, though he admits that he was in bed with her and they were both naked. I did not ask, nor did he tell, what they were doing, though whether they were having intercourse or not was irrelevant. Being naked, in bed, with another girl was not going to go down well with Cynci. I acted poorly and personally told Mike he was out of the band. The band were all together on Mike's porch when I went to Mike's bedroom and told him he was, "a pimp and a shit drummer". (An exact quote according to Jim Cain.) I came out the bedroom followed by an upset Mike, who had tears streaming down his face. Jim jumped up and stood between us to avoid fisticuffs. It was obvious that Mike was crushed, though today he denies it. According to Mike, the day he was let go is also the day he received his drivers license in the mail. Since he could now drive, he wasn't that bothered about being booted. I don't buy that, but have no proof to the contrary. Mike did rejoin The Moving Violation for a while and was briefly a member of the next incarnation, The Red, White and Blues Band, though he seemed to have lost his edge as a drummer. It might have been his drug use, or possibly his passion for women. In a recent conversation Mike claimed that he was booted because he wasn't serious enough about his equipment. He only had a partial kit, lacking a floor tom, and said that band members kept giving him shit about it. At the Bloom battle of the bands Mike had to ask other drummers to borrow a floor drum. He never added extra cymbals or other equipment, while the rest of us were upgrading guitars, amps and p.a. systems. At this time Ginger Baker of Cream had a huge kit of about twenty pieces, while Mike still had five. Mike says he was spending money on drugs and going to concerts such as Cream and Frank Zappa. Whatever the cause of Mike being kicked out, he got on with his life and was soon replaced. I deal with immense guilt to this day.

Further proof of the evolution of The Moving Violation is that our sound was changing, and with it my choice of instruments. I had been playing my 12-string Danelectro, which was great for the jangly folk sound that had been so popular. Now that Jimi Hendrix and Eric Clapton had emerged, jangly folk music was being pushed aside in favor of wailing electric guitars and distortion. As a result I bought a new (used) guitar. A friend from Homewood-Flossmoor, Roger Johnson, had a Fender Jaguar. Fender was famous for its Stratocaster and Telecaster models, and it had introduced the Mustang as a less expensive starter guitar. The Jaguar was designed as a top-end model. Roger's guitar—which had a beautiful blue/green finish—had been purchased new by his guitar teacher, who sold it to Roger. Roger was an easy-going guy who agreed to sell it to me for $175 with $75 up front and the rest paid over the next year. I still have the receipt for the final payment, which was made on November 4, 1968. The action was so much better than on my Danelectro, and I could now play barre chords. It was like swinging a really heavy baseball bat, then picking up a much lighter bat and feeling much, much stronger. The Jaguar was my lighter, faster bat, so to speak. Besides, Fender was my favorite brand, and my playing improved significantly with the purchase.

Greg Stone with Roger Johnson's Fender Jaguar (1966)
This is the very guitar that I bought in Autumn 1967

The 12-string jangle of the Danelectro had been replaced by a serious rock instrument. Along with the Jordon Bosstone that Jim Cain and I had bought, we were able to create a distorted, psychedelic sound. (The following year I sold my Danelectro, a move that distresses me to this day. I'm a collector, and it pains me to not have kept my original guitar that served me so admirably.) With a better rock guitar, a decent amp and extra equipment that allowed me to produce the 'in' sounds of 1968, it was obvious that music and The Moving Violation mattered immensely to me. This doesn't justify booting Steve and Mike, though it may explain where we were coming from. I was so upset by the conflicts with the other two original member—and my oldest friends in The Moving Violation—that I quit in February, though I did return a month later. My replacement, by the way, was a guitarist named Dennis, who became known as D2, with Dennis Montella being D1. My designation as D3 shows how bandmates felt about me when I quit.

With the change in personnel, we felt that a name change was also in order. I suppose we felt that The Moving Violation was a name from our youth (one year earlier!) and wanted something edgier. The blues was very popular in Chicago (Muddy Waters, Buddy Guy, Willie Dixon) and British rockers were huge blues fans. The earliest albums by the Rolling Stones and Cream featured rock versions of old blues tunes by the likes of Robert Johnson. Steve Crosse had added the Paul Butterfield Blues Band song "Born in Chicago" to our set list and started playing harmonica on it and a few other songs. This new direction required a new name, so we rebranded as The Red, White and Blues Band, a name proposed by Steve Crosse. There were apparently some who still thought of us as The Moving Violation. We played four gigs the summer of '68 at Valley View Young Adult Klub (YAK) in Frankfort,

Ill. Valley View, about 15 miles west of Chicago Heights, booked national acts such as Archie Bell and the Drells, Blue Cheer and Mobey Grape. We were usually billed as The Red, White and Blues Band, though once as The Moving Violation.

Red, White and Blues Band: Jim, Dennis, Louie, Gary, Steve

Jim Cain and Gary Harn remained as vocalists with Gary now playing some organ, Steve Crosse sang and played harmonica on a few numbers, and Jim Cain still doubled as guitarist, but other musicians moved in and out. Steve Crosse played some bass, I was temporarily replaced by D2, Mike was replaced on drums by Louie Patrizi who had drummed with The Drakes, co-winners of the Bloom Battle of the Bands, and Danny Freeh (Bad Habits bass player) sat in on bass for the sole Wisconsin gig. The Red, White and Blues Band never had a set lineup and only lasted about five months. Rather than taking off like a rocket for the top, the truth was that after the Bloom Battle of the Bands things slowly slid downhill.

With the help of Dennis Montella, The Red, White and Blues band landed the job in Wisconsin, which was very cool since it was an out-of-state job. I didn't make the trip since I had dropped out of the band. Dennis Montella insisted that the band start with "Born In Chicago". Steve Crosse sang and played harmonica. We also had a few gigs at St. Agnes church and played four times at Valley View. While it lasted, The Red White and Blues Band received raves reviews. Jim Cain had put in lots of practice time and was passing me with his technique. This pushed me to crank up my playing a notch (not as musical rivals, but as colleagues who inspired each other to get better) and together we made a formidable guitar duo. Louie Patrizi was recommended to us by Dennis Montella. Louie was a greaser who a year earlier would probably have preferred beating our punk butts rather than playing with us, but after the battle we had credibility and an apparently bright future; so Louie would wash the grease from his hair (literally) and join us for practice and jobs. Louie was a great drummer and a terrific vocalist as well, so when we did songs like Cream's "I Feel Free", which starts with a 3-part harmony, Louie was huge. In terms of personality, however, Louie was a bust. Steve Crosse does not remember him fondly. Louie pushed his own musical agenda (rhythm and blues) and did not fit in with the other band members. Lee Abrams remembered watching Louie beat somebody to a bloody pulp, something that horrified and frightened the rest of us. Although the band's set list was current with a lot of Cream, Hendrix and Vanilla Fudge, the band was not a tight social unit. How could it be, with the mix of tough Italian greaser and soft, suburban kids.

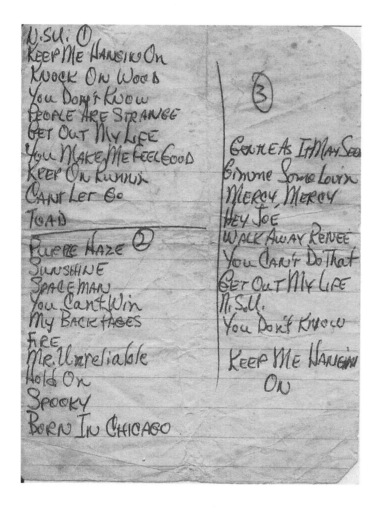

Red, White and Blues Band Set List

In spite of our potential, it was obvious that The Red, White and Blues band was reaching the end. That end was hastened when Steve Crosse showed up completely wasted at our final show at Valley View YAK, August 31. Steve had lost his dad at an early age, and he and his mother had developed a combative relationship that led to constant shouting matches. Those who visited Steve at home got used to it, but it was a demented scene. Possibly, as a consequence, Steve became a substance abuser. As we were setting up, Steve stumbled in completely messed up on what he told us later was a particularly potent type of

LSD known as Orange Wedge. (LSD—acid as it was called—had groovy names like Purple Double Domes and Orange Sunshine.) Steve was so out of it he couldn't even tune his bass, and didn't get up on stage.

At this time an event occurred that would lead me to take off an entire year from being in a band. Jim Cain and I went to a dance at a tennis court (very common in those days) that featured Bangor Flying Circus. We spotted two pretty young ladies, though Jim and I were too shy to approach them. Fortunately, the two beauties approached us. Mary Aagesen and Debby Voytovich were in a band called The Distractions, an all-girl band that did excellent covers of, among others, the Jefferson Airplane and Etta James.

The Distractions with Debby and Mary on the left

98

Debby and I became an item, as they used to say. She went to Rich East High School, so I spent a lot of time riding my bike to meet her, me not owning a car. The relationship soon became our main interest and music fell by the wayside. The drummer of The Distractions still blames me on her Facebook page for The Distractions breaking up, but I feel no guilt. Nothing beats young love, and I had already gotten a great buzz from being in a band. My senior year was devoted to Debby Voytovich, my first love, and I have absolutely no regrets. I didn't miss band politics and personal conflicts and fear of union thugs, I had something better happening.

As the Byrds sang, you don't miss your water 'til the well runs dry. Some memories fade over time, but The Moving Violation seemed to grow in importance. Years later I began to appreciate the special thing we created in 1967. The six members of The Moving Violation weren't best friends, but we shared an experience that stayed with us—for good or bad, in one form or another—for the rest of our lives. The Bloom Battle of the Bands did not lead to fame and fortune. It was, however, one of those moments that helped shape the lives of seven young men (including Lee Abrams). It gave us the sense that we could achieve anything if we set our minds to it. Today, 45 years later, all of the members of The Moving Violation retain vivid memories of the battle. I wish that every young person could achieve one simple moment of glory, one episode or event that confirms the fact that, in their own way, they are special.

EPILOGUE

In the fall of 1969, having graduated from Homewood-Flossmoor, I enrolled at Prairie State Junior College. I did well there the first year and still had my girlfriend so I was content. I wasn't in a band, but I played guitar almost every day and I knew I was getting better. The summer of '70 was spent going to concerts and music festivals, and also hooking back up with Mike Kennedy and Steve Small, who was home for summer vacation. My girlfriend Debby went away to college in autumn of '70 and we stopped seeing each other. Steve returned to Brown University, and Mike moved to Denver in late summer, 1971. When it looked like I might get drafted into the army (my draft number was 8, meaning a very high likelihood of being drafted!) I took off for Providence, Rhode Island, to see Steve Small at Brown. We were good friends, yet one of my main reasons for going to Brown was that it was closer to Canada in case I was called into the army. (I was morally opposed to the Vietnam War and had decided to head north if I was drafted.) I eventually returned to Chicago, took my military physical, and passed it in spite of high blood pressure. For the next year I played a delaying game since eligibility only lasts for one year after passing your physical. I kept writing my draft board, challenging my medical status, then informing them I was moving to Denver, then telling them I had again returned to Chicago. It took so long for my draft board to reply that these correspondences lasted the entire year, by which time my draft eligibility had expired and I no longer had the army waiting to take me.

I moved to Denver in March, '72, with the plan of starting a country-rock band, like The New Riders of the Purple Sage, with Steve Small on pedal steel (during his summer vacations and after he graduated) and possibly Mike Kennedy on drums along with a couple of his friends. We did have some success playing music together, but not for long. In '75 I moved up to Evergreen, which is in the foothills west of Denver. I was still playing in a band with Mike Kennedy at this time but Steve, who had moved to Colorado after graduating in 1973, left in '75 to travel around Europe. In need of a steady income (which is rare for a musician) I started working for Jefferson County Schools as a bus driver, then as a custodian and finally as a HVAC tech. I stayed with Jefferson County for 31 years.

In 1979 I met the love of my life, Ann Dam. The thing that brought us together was, naturally, music. She wanted to learn to play and, when I heard that she had Grateful Dead reel-to-reel tapes, that sealed the deal. I had briefly stopped playing music, but with her inspiration I started playing again. We bought Ann her own electric guitar and amp, and soon she became an accomplished rhythm guitarist and vocalist. Over the years we have had many groups with the two of us as the nucleus. Currently Ann and I are playing in a group called The Rhubarb Project that includes my neighbor Tom Chart from across the street on keyboards and, of course, my co-author R J Furth on bass guitar. Ann and I write original music, and we play tasty covers as well including many Grateful Dead tunes and songs by The Beatles, Joni Mitchell, Bob Dylan and other groups from the 60s, 70s and 80s.

I strongly feel that if not for music and the early success of my music, my life would have turned out way different. I am grateful that I can still play and enjoy music in my life. It somehow completes me as a person and I still see it as an adventure. I feel fortunate that I can play with good friends and still make beautiful music. That's what it is all about!

During the past year R J and I have met with all of the surviving band members of The Moving Violation (Denver, Chicago, St. Louis) as well as Lee Abrams. Below are brief summaries of their lives after The Moving Violation.

JIM CAIN. Jim ended up marrying his high school girlfriend and they had three children together. Sadly, the marriage did not last. Jim stopped playing music, instead focusing his energy on his children and working as an industrial pipe designer for several companies in and around Chicago. He currently lives outside of Chicago with his second wife Carmen and has returned to one of his great passions: guitars. Jim now designs outstanding acoustic and electric guitars. Check out his work at Jim Cain Guitars. I have one of his Telecaster models (based on the Fender Telecaster) and it is a great instrument. It has been a pleasure to be back in contact with Jim. We have met up in Denver and, most recently, at his home in Chicago. His wife Carmen, by the way, is a dynamite cook.

STEVE CROSSE. I hung out a lot with Steve in 1970 and the later part of '71, then I moved to Colorado. Steve's mother and sister moved to Boulder in 1974 and Steve moved to the Denver area shortly thereafter. He played in a few bands in Denver in the late 70s as well as the next few decades. Today he lives in Golden, Colorado, and is geographically the closet member of The Moving Violation to me. Although Steve no longer plays music, he is still very much a hip music aficionado.

GARY HARN. Gary was drafted into the army about 1970 but didn't stay in very long because of flat feet. Since many young American men were being sent to Vietnam at that time it was perhaps fortunate. After exiting the army Gary took up drumming as well as keyboards and played in various bands around the Chicago area for several years. I lost contact with him until 2011, at which time we began communicating online. Unfortunately, I never had the chance to meet up again with Gary as he passed away in early 2012 from heart trouble. I deeply regret not keeping up with Gary through the years. Although all of the members of The Moving Violation were nice people, Gary was perhaps the nicest. He got along with everybody, with the exception of Bob Schmit, and was never part of the ugly band politics that led to the breakup of The Moving Violation.

MIKE KENNEDY. Mike graduated in 1969 from Bloom and we hung out together in 1970, going to music festivals in the Midwest. The conflicts that led to Mike's departure from The Moving Violations rapidly faded and we were able to continue our friendship. Mike moved to Denver in late summer of '71 and has lived there ever since. He was the drummer of the Frank Hart Band, a band that both Steve Small and I were part of in Denver in the early 70s. Mike was also the drummer of the band I was in after the Frank Hart Band. That band, called Big Frank, lasted for only a few months and was over by the summer of '75. In the late

70s Mike had a small restaurant in south Denver called South Pearl Eats. He no longer owns the restaurant. Mike started a family in the early 80s and today he enjoys his grandchildren and is still into music, though he doesn't play anymore. Mike works for the US Postal Service.

STEVE SMALL. Steve finished his senior year at Bloom running on the cross country and track teams. He was accepted at Brown University (because of his grades and his running, not his bass playing), graduated in 1973, and moved to Denver where we started The Frank Hart Band. By that time he was learning how to play the pedal steel guitar and was no longer playing bass. Because of our interest in the Grateful Dead we both had turned to Country-Rock music and were infatuated with The New Riders of the Purple Sage. Jerry Garcia was playing pedal steel guitar with The New Riders and was a major influence on both of us. In 1975 Steve traveled to Germany as a delayed graduation present to himself. When he returned to Denver he played pedal steel with Gary Morris in a band called Breakaway. Gary got signed to a record deal, moved to Nashville, and left his band in Denver. Steve went back to Germany and played pedal steel with country bands from '78 through '79 and then moved back to Denver. (Steve's country and western band had a hit in Germany!) In 1984 Steve moved to Nashville and became Gary Morris's manager until the early 90s. Steve worked as manager for various ventures like the Belacourt Theater in Nashville and currently works as production manager of TNA Impact Wrestling.

LEE ABRAMS. (This is mostly taken from Lee's citation in Wikipedia.) In the 1970s as FM radio took off Lee worked for radio stations. His main innovation was the "Superstars of Rock and Roll" format designed to appeal to a demographic of white males aged between 12 and 24. Along with his partner Kent Burkhart he introduced the format to more than 100 stations across America. This format favored white rock acts like Led Zeppelin. Most recently Lee was the chief innovation officer for the Tribune Company (2008-2010) but prior to that founded XM Satellite Radio and served as Chief Programming Officer at that company until his departure in 2008, founded and ran notable radio consulting company Burkhart/Abrams, served as an internal consultant for ABC Radio, and helped develop nationwide radio formats such as Z-Rock and Radio Disney. Additionally, he has been involved on the recording side of the music industry, producing *Ah Via Musicom* for guitarist Eric Johnson and appearing on several Alan Parsons Project CDs. He has also consulted and managed acts such as Yes, The Moody Blues, Steve Winwood, Iron Maiden, and Bob Seger. Lee's latest project is TouchVision, the online 21st century news source.

Made in the USA
San Bernardino, CA
26 April 2014